GW00370727

LOCKDOWN
LUNCHEONS

PUBLISHED BY
LUNCHEON EDITIONS, 2021

Edible Arrangement by photographer Annie Collinge, 2020 (see pp.42-43)

LOCKDOWN LUNCHEONS 2020/21

In March 2020, as we in the UK realised we were to be locked up in our first lockdown, many people turned to cooking to soothe their anxieties, sharing their creations online rather than around a table. I started to write to friends and contributors to *Luncheon*, asking them to offer a suggestion for a lunch that could be comforting and easily made while in isolation, to be shared daily on our Instagram account. They are gathered here as a memento of 2020, with new ones created specially during the second lockdown of 2021. The recipes, photographs, paintings and illustrations have been created by designers, poets, cooks, writers, photographers and artists, with beautiful and personal stories of where the recipes originated, what they mean to each person, or who they would love to cook for when everyone can meet and eat together again.

Each contributor has selected a food or community organisation for which they would like to raise awareness, and running through the issue are advertisements created by artists for the London-based community project Poot It In Yer Bag, founded by Elaine Chalmers (please read her text on p.32). This special edition of *Luncheon* is a small response to these very challenging and unprecedented times. Thank you so very much to everyone who has contributed a Lockdown Luncheon and to those who helped to make this booklet.

Frances
Editor of *Luncheon* magazine

CONTRIBUTORS INDEX

Sandwich Cake for an indoor picnic, see pp.152–153.
Recipe and photograph by Anna Nevala and Josefine Skomars, 2021

MAMMA ANDERSSON & JOCKUM NORDSTRÖM

Stockholms Stadsmission
Stockholm, Sweden

March was so weird and scary, even though Sweden was much more open than other countries. We were isolated from all friends, restaurants, cinemas, galleries, cafés and everything else that makes life fun and nice outside of the studio. But we worked a lot. I was very focused in my studio; nothing disturbed me. Every morning I did a workout in front of the television for 20 minutes. Then breakfast and after that a walk with Aslan to my studio.

It's the day before Easter. This type of meal is very simple, traditional Swedish food, made to celebrate Easter, Christmas and Midsummer. It's normally eaten more like a starter before the main course. And when you have a big celebration meal, you have many different styles of herring on the table. You can make them to your own recipe using different pickle ingredients, vinegars and spices. But today we had simple cans from the supermarket. It's just me and Jockum with our dog Aslan, our cat Tottoro and Ulo Ulo our tortoise.

ON THE TABLE IS:
boiled potatoes
matjessill herrings
soured cream with chives
tomatoes
radishes
crisp breads with Västerbotten cheese
butter
snaps and vodka, alcohol-free beer

The dessert is coffee and a coconut ball.

ANFEARGORM

Convento dei Frati Cappuccini Redentore
Venice, Italy

Ireland, 2018

Ireland, 2021

Once, long ago, while staying with the brothers at the monastery of la Grande Chartreuse in France, I remember eating in SILENCE a dish of such humble simplicity that to this day it remains etched into my memory.

INGREDIENTS
1 large turnip
2 tablespoons sugar
2 bay leaves
1 teaspoon salt
200ml cream
a good knob of country butter
1 teaspoon black pepper (or pepper dillisk)

DIRECTIONS
Peel and chop the turnip and place in a saucepan with the sugar, bay leaves and salt. Top up with water to cover the turnip, bring to the boil and cook until tender. Drain and roughly mash the turnip, adding the cream, butter and pepper. Place in an ovenproof dish and cook under the grill until golden and bubbling.

ANTHONY ATLAS

Citymeals on Wheels
New York City, United States

During lockdown I found myself marvelling at a relic from my grandfather's old business: a vintage bottle of Sam Milchman Health Seltzer. My grandfather, Sam Milchman, was a Jewish émigré from Poland who survived forced internment at an ammunitions factory during WWII. After he moved to the United States, he started a soda business and delivered seltzer to homes in Brooklyn throughout the 1950s and 1960s. It occurred to me how the business would be thriving if it were still in operation today, dropping off health seltzer to people isolated in their homes throughout the city.

For lunch, I turn to the Hot Miso Tuna Sandwich, which is easy to make with pantry items and is a reflection of the kind of Japanese-American hybrid comfort food I love. I think of it as something one might enjoy with seltzer or coffee, or packed for lunch while on seltzer delivery. It's presented here in the living room of my apartment where, in another room, I host The Middler, an apartment gallery.

HOT MISO TUNA SANDWICH

INGREDIENTS
1 tin of sustainably caught tuna, drained
2 tablespoons red or white miso
mirin, tamari and cooking sake, to taste
a knob of butter
2 slices of Udi's gluten-free white bread
Kewpie mayonnaise
togarashi

DIRECTIONS
Mash the tuna thoroughly with a generous heap of miso, at least 2 tablespoons. Add a splash of mirin for moisture. Heat a cast iron frying pan with a little oil and, when hot, add the tuna in a flat layer, turning it over in the oil so it is evenly coated. Cook the tuna for 8 minutes or so, adding a splash of tamari and cooking sake for moisture and sweetness. Flip and mix the tuna every few minutes until it is evenly browned, almost crisping.

In another pan, melt the butter over a medium heat and add the slices of bread. Cook until golden, then turn and cook the other sides. When ready, assemble your sandwich with a side of Kewpie mayo and togarashi.

ADEJOKÉ BAKARE

Oxford Homeless Project
Oxford, United Kingdom

Photograph by Nic Crilly-Hargrave, 2021

Kedjenou is a light chicken and vegetable stew, traditionally cooked in a tightly closed earthenware pot, which causes the chicken to steam and pressure-cook at the same time. The chicken cooks in its own juices, resulting in flesh that is moist and intensely flavoured. Dambu is the name for a variety of side dishes made from either broken rice or millet. It can be an accompaniment for stews or sauces, but it's also delicious eaten on its own.

CHICKEN KEDJENOU

INGREDIENTS

1 small chicken or 8 chicken thighs

3 tablespoons lemon juice

3 tablespoons vegetable oil

1 onion, diced

2 tablespoons minced ginger

2 garlic cloves

1 red pepper, diced

Scotch bonnet chilli, chopped (to taste)

1 bay leaf

1 teaspoon ground star anise

2 pods of grains of selim (uda) (optional)

1 teaspoon ground white pepper

salt

DIRECTIONS

Rub the chicken all over with 2 tablespoons of the lemon juice, 1 tablespoon of salt and 2 tablespoons of the vegetable oil, then leave to marinate for 2-6 hours.

Heat a little oil in a frying pan and brown the chicken to give colour to the skin. In a heavy based pan, fry the onion, ginger and garlic in a little more oil for 5 minutes. Add the red pepper, chilli, spices and seasoning to the pan and arrange the chicken on top. Put foil over the top of the pan and cover it tightly with the lid. Cook over a gentle heat for 1 hour. Adjust the seasoning, adding more lemon juice and salt to taste. Serve with the Millet Dambu. Serves 2-4.

MILLET DAMBU

INGREDIENTS

2 tablespoons vegetable oil

100g millet

200ml chicken stock

2 tablespoons lemon juice

1 teaspoon yaji spice (or a pinch each of ground cumin, cloves and dried ginger)

85g moringa or kale, finely chopped and massaged with a pinch of salt

40g carrots, shredded

1 small onion, finely chopped

40g peanuts or pumpkin seeds, toasted

salt

DIRECTIONS

Heat a heavy based pan, add 1 tablespoon of oil and fry the millet grains, stirring constantly to avoid burning. When the grains all turn white, add the stock. Cover the pan and cook for 20 minutes, until al dente. Let the millet cool, covered. Mix the lemon juice with 1 tablespoon of oil and the spice and add to the millet. Mix well. Add the vegetables, season to taste, garnish with the nuts and serve.

MAX BELLHOUSE

Dinner is Served
London, United Kingdom

Schnitzel Time by Tilly Power, 2020

SCHNITZEL

INGREDIENTS

1 chicken breast, pork loin steak or veal
 escalope
flour
1 egg, beaten
a handful of breadcrumbs
oil or a knob of butter
salt and pepper

DIRECTIONS

Place the meat between two sheets of baking paper and bash with a meat mallet or heavy object to flatten. Dust in seasoned flour, dip in the beaten egg then coat in the breadcrumbs. Heat a large frying pan with a little oil or butter and fry the schnitzel until golden on both sides and cooked through. Serve with a cucumber or potato salad and a glass of beer.

Painting by Magnus Reid for Poot It In Yer Bag, 2021
Read more about the Poot It In Yer Bag project on page 32.

PATCHARAVIPA BODIRATNANGKURA

Foundation for Slum Child Care
Bangkok, Thailand

POMELO SALAD

Here's my great grandmother Khun Ying Sin's recipe for Pomelo Salad from the 1930s:

INGREDIENTS
100g shredded pomelo
15g shredded boiled chicken breast
2 large cooked prawns, cut in half
25g dried coconut flakes
15g soft brown sugar
8g roasted peanuts, crushed
20ml lime juice
5g crispy fried red onions
1–2 coriander leaves
2 pieces of dried chilli
salt and pepper

DIRECTIONS
Place the pomelo, chicken, prawns, coconut, sugar and peanuts in a mixing bowl, season generously with salt and pepper and mix gently. Add the lime juice and mix again. Add the fried onions, mix one more time then pile on a plate. Decorate your dish with coriander and dried chilli. Enjoy!

JACKSON BOXER

Migrateful

United Kingdom

FRIED PORK CHOP, COURGETTES & LEEKS OVER STEAMED RICE

These wonderful Tamworth chops, when grilled in a hot skillet, release so much rich fat they end up shallow frying in their own lard, giving them a beautiful crisp, almost lacquered crust. I rest them when they're coloured all over but not quite cooked through, with an internal temperature of about 145°F, and allow them to gently relax.

Meanwhile I sautée sliced leeks and courgettes in the fat in the pan, deglazing with good cider vinegar, white soy sauce and a squeeze of lemon juice, then frying hard until the vegetables are coloured but not yet collapsed and the juices have combined into a lovely brown pan sauce. After seasoning, it is acceptable to sweeten with a pinch of sugar to soften the astringency of all the vinegar necessary to cut through the richness of all the fat – this is a pretty unapologetic plate of food. Serve over warm steamed rice.

KATIE BURNETT

Meals on Wheels of Greater St. Louis
St. Louis, United States

Photographs by Katie Burnett from her book *Cabin Fever*
(Art Paper Editions, 2021)

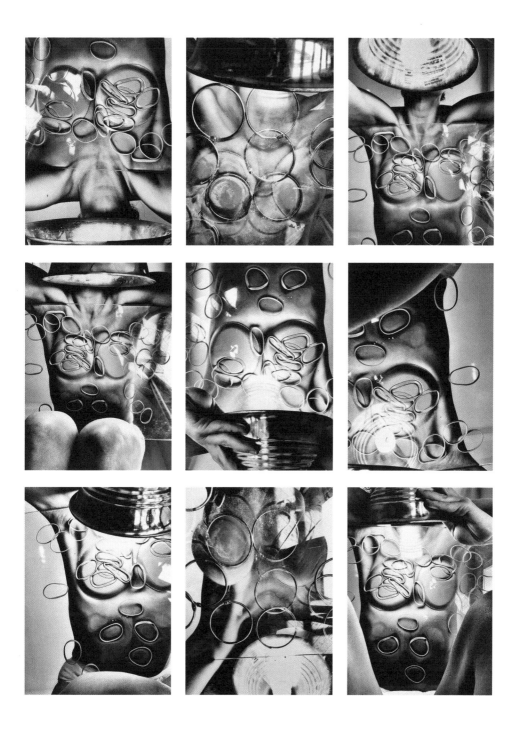

GARETH CASEY

BAPIF: Banque Alimentaire de Paris et d'Île de France
Paris and Île-de-France region, France

My grandmother used to make all her own bread in her rickety, cast iron wood-burning oven. With any leftover dough, she would make a special treat – any leftover food in the fridge, be it cooked vegetables or meat, was wrapped and weaved into the long strips of leftover dough, baked and served with rich gravy, gooey cheese or soup.

Here is my own meager attempt, baked during lockdown, with leftover roasted vegetables from the night before.

'WASTE NOT, WANT NOT' BREAD

INGREDIENTS

480g plain flour
40g wheat semolina
15g dried yeast
10g salt
50g olive oil
320g water
leftover roasted vegetables
a handful of seeds or grains

DIRECTIONS

Place the flour and semolina in a mixing bowl, add the yeast and salt and mix well. Add the oil and water, then bring together to make a dough. Knead on a lightly floured surface for 10–15 minutes then leave covered with a dry towel in a warm room to rise for 1½ hours.

Rework it lightly to get some of the air out of it, then pull on the dough to make long strips, about 50–60cm in length, and lay them on a floured surface. Take your roasted vegetables, with or without meat scraps, then wrap them with the bands of dough, weaving the dough in between the leftovers. You should end up with a big ball of dough, interlaced with vegetables sticking out on all sides. Scatter over seeds or grains of your choice, then place on a baking sheet and cook in a hot oven at 250°C for 25 minutes, placing it low in the oven so the top does not burn.

Let the loaf cool a little, then eat while still warm with gooey cheese. This makes enough for 4, but mine only lasted for 30 minutes after coming out of the oven and there were only 2 of us.

Thank you Nana.

ROSE
CHALALAI SINGH

Food for Soul
Italy (with global network)

CHILLED ALMOND SOUP

This recipe is made with fresh almonds, but you could also use dried almonds. If you have dried almonds, soak them in water for one or two hours, then take the brown skins off. You will also need to double the amount of water in the recipe.

INGREDIENTS
150g fresh blanched almonds
125ml cold water
1–2 garlic gloves, depending on how strong
    you want the garlic flavour to be
60ml extra virgin olive oil
salt and black pepper

DIRECTIONS
Place the almonds, water, garlic and olive oil together in a blender and blend at high speed until the soup becomes milky and smooth... add another drop of olive oil, salt and black pepper before serving.

ELAINE CHALMERS

Poot It In Yer Bag, supporting Children with Voices
London, United Kingdom

I chose this salad as I'm longing for summer and I just love salads. But more importantly, I have recently set up a project called Poot It In Yer Bag and decided to partner with a charity providing food for vulnerable families in our community of Hackney, called Children with Voices.

Each week we get food donations and have to choose what to cook. Sometimes it's quite a challenge but I think we do pretty well. We manage to produce about 100 meals for the hub, which we deliver, and also have a soup kitchen in the local pub, The Spurstowe Arms, who have kindly donated their kitchen. We also supply a local school with over 40 boxes of fruit, vegetables, drinks and dry goods, so it's pretty close to my heart.

ROAST BEETROOT, PICKLED CARROT & RASPBERRY SALAD

INGREDIENTS

6 beetroots, scrubbed
4 garlic cloves, unpeeled
1 sprig of thyme
4 tablespoons olive oil, plus extra for drizzling
1 bunch of watercress
2 heads of red chicory, separated into leaves
a handful of toasted pine nuts
a few pickled carrots
a squeeze of lemon juice
1 ball of burrata, if you fancy
Raspberry Vinaigrette (see below)
salt and pepper

DIRECTIONS

Place the beetroot, garlic, thyme and olive oil in a roasting tin, toss to coat in the oil and cook in the oven at 180°C for 1½ hours, turning occasionally, until tender. Allow to cool a little, then peel and slice the beetroot and pop the garlic from its skin. Season to taste.

Place the watercress, chicory, pine nuts and pickled carrots in a bowl, season with salt and pepper and drizzle with a little oil and a squeeze of lemon juice. Place the sliced beetroot on a plate and top with the salad and the burrata, if you fancy it. Drizzle the raspberry vinaigrette over the salad. Eat and enjoy. This is enough for 4.

RASPBERRY VINAIGRETTE

INGREDIENTS

125g raspberries
75ml olive oil
40ml red wine vinegar
½ teaspoon Dijon mustard
salt and pepper

DIRECTIONS

Place the ingredients in a food processor, whizz for 30 seconds, then pass through a sieve. Season to taste.

POOT IT IN YER BAG

I set up this project in response to the Government's meagre £30 box of food offered to vulnerable families each week during lockdown. I started contacting all the local restaurants and businesses around Hackney and the response was immense. I also contacted The Spurstowe Arms to ask if I could use their kitchen, and Naomi agreed.

I wanted to partner up with the Children with Voices charity run by Michelle Dornelly – what an amazing woman! So I got in touch and the rest is history.

I contacted my old friend Dennis, who used to own Bill Bean fruit and veg for many years but now runs Fruve London. He was so up for helping, in fact he is the reason we have managed to keep going. Dennis has been delivering every Friday with the most amazing goods, ranging from fruit and vegetables to drinks, pasta, tinned goods and chocolate.

We have had produce from many local businesses, including Leila's, Bistrotheque, the Dusty Knuckle Bakery, the TowPath Café, Lardo, Allpress Espresso, Violet Cakes, Voodoo Ray's and London Borough of Jam, to name a few – the list is endless. We do donations day on Saturday at the pub, a free kitchen on Monday, local school food boxes and deliveries of shopping to local people. We just produced 500 school meals for half term with the help of all our volunteers. We also do cook-offs on Sunday and Wednesday, making prepared meals to be taken to the Community hubs, along with the dry goods, fruit and vegetables.

In addition, we have set up a PayPal account for the charity. With the help of Cate Halpin we have managed to get local artists on board to do a drawing or doodle for our Instagram. Eventually we will have a show and sell the work, further helping to fund our charity. You can see some of the works running through this book.

It's what I call COMMUNITY.

Elaine Chalmers

Sweet Peas by Little Fish Design for Poot It In Yer Bag, 2021
Read more about the Poot It In Yer Bag project opposite.

ZANNE CHAUDHRY

Oxford Homeless Project
Oxford, United Kingdom

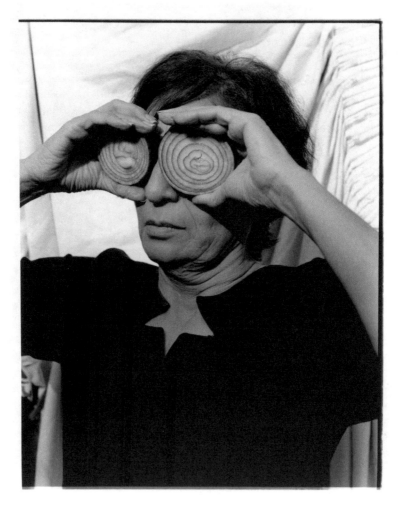

Aloo Gobi, A Family Tradition,
photographed by Zanne Chaudhry, 2021

It's the 7 March 2021 and I'm speaking to my mother, Farhat Chaudhry, about Aloo Gobi, my chosen recipe for lunch.

ME: So Mum, what are the ingredients for Aloo Gobi?

MUM: The main ingredients are cauliflower, potato, onions, tomato and coriander.

ME: What about the spices?

MUM: Spices are red chilli, salt, turmeric, cumin seeds, garam masala and ginger.

ME: Did you used to have it as a kid in Pakistan?

MUM: Yes

ME: In the village in Vehari?

MUM: Yes, my mother used to make it.

ME: With roti?

MUM: Yes, mostly roti.

ME: Which is chapati. And no rice?

MUM: Mostly dry curry is eaten with chapati, not rice.

ME: I feel like vegetarian curries derive from India, because they eat Indian dishes in Pakistan?

MUM: Dishes from India and Pakistan are the same basically, not much difference. Pakistan was in India before, so all the recipes are shared.

ME: Did your mother eat it when she was young as well?

MUM: Yes, I think so.

ME: Why have I always loved Aloo Gobi?

MUM: Because you can eat it with a paratha!

ME: So explain what Aloo Gobi Paratha is.

MUM: So basically, when you make this dry curry at night, then you can mash it and put it inside the chapati.

ME: So you put the Aloo Gobi as a filling in a chapati and deep fry it?

MUM: No, not deep fry, it's cooked on a pan like a pancake.

ME: I ate too many, I can't eat any more – they are so heavy. I think Aloo Gobi 's got quite a funny name; maybe that's why I like it.

MUM: Yes, it's the kind of thing referenced in films as well, like in *Bend It Like Beckham* – 'What kind of daughter are you if you can't even cook Aloo Gobi?!'

ME: Why do you think they used that dish?

MUM: It's quite a simple dish…and if you can't even cook that…

ME: I remember the first time I cooked it when I was not living at home. I forgot to put the tomato in it, it was very yellow.

MUM: Yes, you have to have a tomato or half a tin of tomatoes in it. Well, there we have it – the legendary Aloo Gobi.

SAM AND
SAM CLARK

The Lighthouse Project
London, United Kingdom

We have to admit, we have not always been fans of the Egyptian staple, ful (slow-cooked spiced fava beans). In the same way that broad beans are an acquired taste for kids, ful is too. But now we are converted, we are evangelists! A fresh, simple and nutritious lunch, with flatbread as the tool to scoop it up.

We are huge fans of Hodmedods, a company that champions and supplies pulses, grains and flours from British farms. Interestingly, the fava bean has been grown in Britain since the Iron Age. All the more reason to celebrate the British fava bean with its culinary roots in Ancient Egypt.

FUL MEDAMES

INGREDIENTS

3 tablespoons olive oil

2 leeks, excess green removed, washed and chopped

3 garlic cloves, sliced

1 teaspoon cumin seeds, dry roasted over a medium heat and ground

1 teaspoon ground coriander

⅓ teaspoon freshly ground black pepper

1 fresh green chilli, finely chopped

6 cherry tomatoes, diced

2 x 400g tins of cooked pulses (ideally fava beans but chickpeas or lentils amply suffice)

salt

TO SERVE

Chopped Salad (see below)

Tahini Sauce (see below)

posh olive oil, to finish

sliced green chilli

warm pita or flatbreads

DIRECTIONS

Place the oil, leeks, garlic, cumin, coriander, pepper and green chilli in a medium-large saucepan and cook over a medium heat for 25 minutes, stirring occasionally. If a little caramelization takes place, all the better. Add the tomatoes and salt and cook for a further 5 minutes. Add the pulses and their liquid to the pan and gently bring to the boil, stirring slowly. Take off the heat.

At home, we purée about a third of the beans with a hand blender, but you can use a potato masher equally well. Top up cautiously with boiling water so the beans are coated with their velvety sauce. Fold in some good olive oil and check for seasoning.

To serve, spoon the warm ful onto 4 plates, scatter over the chopped salad, drizzle with the tahini sauce and finally sprinkle over some extra green chilli and olive oil. Serve with warm pita or flatbread on the side. Serves 4.

CHOPPED SALAD

INGREDIENTS

1 small red onion, finely diced
1 cucumber, peeled and finely diced
10 cherry tomatoes, halved and finely diced
2 tablespoons roughly chopped mint, parsley
   and coriander
½ garlic clove, crushed to a paste with salt
a squeeze of lemon juice
1 tablespoon red wine vinegar
4 tablespoons extra virgin olive oil
salt and pepper

DIRECTIONS

Put all the ingredients in a bowl. Toss well
and season with salt and pepper. Chill for a
fresher taste.

TAHINI SAUCE

INGREDIENTS

1 small garlic clove, crushed to a paste
   with salt
3 tablespoons tahini
juice of ½ lemon
3 tablespoons olive oil
5 tablespoons water
salt and pepper

DIRECTIONS

Place all the ingredients in a jug, season with
a pinch of salt and black pepper and blend
with a hand blender until smooth. Check
for seasoning.

Odysseus and Circe by Nick Wapplington for Poot It In Yer Bag, 2021
Read more about the Poot It In Yer Bag project on page 32.

SADIE COLES

North Paddington Food Bank
London, United Kingdom

Tricky for me as I don't eat lunch, so this is Lockdown Dinner. This is a dal made from a recipe sent to me during the week of lockdown when I got trapped in a web of round-robin poetry and recipe exchanges. The dal recipe caught my eye for its limited list of ingredients, and I like proteins and love dal but had never made it. Now, in lockdown, I am making it once a week and serve it with whatever leftover vegetables I have to hand.

Today I am making it while listening to the live Met Opera Gala, recommended to me by Elizabeth Peyton. Superstar singers and musicians are performing in their homes. The parts with the whole orchestra and chorus are incredibly moving and powerful. It's a living example of the connectivity and vitality of culture in this new digital reality. I always have music on when I am cooking.

Often, like tonight, I cook two meals, one for me and one for my son (he had bolognese tonight, the Marcella Hazan recipe which Fergus Henderson told me was the ONLY one). It keeps life interesting, although I won't be sorry when the 'three meals a day' catering department gets a bit of a rest.

Dal seems to be a favourite for many people, along with chocolate, while we all isolate. Neil Tennant gave his recipe for dal in his 'Answers from Isolation', my Instagram project. A very good recipe. People seem to like the project a lot, in part because it expands outside of my gallery programme. I suppose that is what I am finding interesting about isolation so far. We are inside, detached, but are finding new ways to connect to both our familiar communities and far beyond. I find a lot of hope in that.

ANNIE COLLINGE

The Boiler House N16
London, United Kingdom

Photograph by Annie Collinge, 2020

EDIBLE ARRANGEMENT

INGREDIENTS

2 Mini Babybel cheeses (one purple, one red)
black olives in brine
2 wooden skewers
1 mini cabbage
cooking string
1 turkey slice
green olives in brine
4 cauliflower florets pickled with beetroot
carrot juice for the vase

DIRECTIONS

Using a sharp knife, cut criss-cross patterns in the wax of the cheeses, prise apart the sections and pull out to make the flower petals. Thinly slice olives to make the centres of the flowers and secure to the cheeses with small pieces of skewer. Stick the cheeses onto skewers and tie on cabbage leaves with cooking string to make the leaves.

Scrunch the slice of turkey around a single black olive and secure with cooking string. Arrange green olives all the way up a skewer for the stem. Break up pieces of the pickled cauliflower and thread onto a skewer, then arrange all the skewers in a small vase. Pour in carrot juice to hide the sticks in the vase and to add colour. Serve to yourself or whomever you are self-isolating with.

JASPER CONRAN

Feeding Britain
United Kingdom

Illustration by Jasper Conran, 2021

Letter to a friend

It has been a long time since we have been allowed to meet. A year. It has felt like being on an endless ocean voyage without ever seeing land in sight. However, I count myself lucky in that I managed to skip town early and have been here in the country with a dog, chickens and my beloved. I am painfully aware of the disparity between my experience and most others so you won't hear a peep of complaint out of me, not now, not ever. I have been able to keep myself cheerful on days when clouds have been leaden, thinking about you. Our friendship has managed to span four decades. Years and years of unwavering support and love for which I am VERY grateful. We have travelled the world together for one reason or another and my memories are coloured primarily by the way that you have made me laugh. Not just laugh, but full-on tears down the face, pee-inducing uncontrollable MIRTH. This, along with a hug and a kiss, I think is worth more than all of Solomon's gold, pearls, rubies, emeralds and diamonds. The good news is that there seems to be an end in sight and I am planning for the day when we will see each other again. We can't know exactly when that will be; however, it will be a perfect summer's day. The sky will be cloudless, the sun will be shining, there will be daisies in the grass, woodpigeons cooing in the trees and grass snakes shall frolic in the compost. I shall put a blue checked cloth on the table under the apple tree.

This is what we shall have for our lunch. 1. Roasted red, orange and yellow peppers with garlic and anchovy fillets. I have discovered a website called Vinegar Shed and their Portuguese anchovies are a REVELATION. This has the recommendation of not only being delicious but extremely pretty to look at. 2. Because I love you, I will spend hours and hours making a lobster bisque. This reminds me of my father who could sometimes be found rooting around in the dustbin after lunch, recovering carelessly discarded lobster shells in order that he could have his favourite soup, loudly muttering about waste and the war. It involves a considerable amount of work making fish stock and chicken stock, roasting and pulverizing shells, straining and simmering and what have you, but the result is utterly delicious. We will eat this with sourdough bread straight out of the Aga. 3. Then we shall have a green salad and a slice of Pont l'Evêque, perfectly soft and tasty and redolent of an Elizabeth David picnic. 4. I don't really know why, but jelly in nearly all its forms makes me happy and so, to finish off, I shall serve you a big wobbly booby orange jelly. Naturally we shall have had several glasses of wine, both before and during our meal, and I imagine that we shall drift off into a snooze for an hour or two before resuming where we left off.

GRILLED PEPPER SALAD

If you are using whole salted anchovies, use six of them, rinse to wash off the salt, scrape off the silver skin and fillet them to make 12 fillets. Capers can also be used to dress this dish.

INGREDIENTS

6 sweet peppers
12 anchovy fillets
3 garlic cloves, finely chopped
3 tablespoons finely chopped parsley
4 tablespoons olive oil
2 teaspoons lemon juice

TO DRESS

black pepper
lemon juice
finely chopped garlic
finely chopped parsley

DIRECTIONS

Scorch the peppers under a hot grill, turning from time to time, until their skins are blackened and blistered all over. Place inside a sealed bag to cool or plunge into a bowl of cold water for a few minutes. The skins should now come off quite easily. Slice the peppers in half, remove the pith and rinse out the seeds under cold running water. Pat them dry and cut in quarters.

Slice the anchovy fillets in half along their length. Combine them in a serving dish with the peppers and toss lightly with the chopped garlic and parsley. Heat the olive oil and lemon juice in a small pan. When hot, pour over the peppers, lightly mix and leave to cool.

Dress with pepper, more lemon juice, chopped garlic and chopped parsley before serving. Add salt only if necessary.

LOBSTER BISQUE

INGREDIENTS

2 live lobsters, each weighing around 700g

125g unsalted butter

1 carrot, diced

1 onion, diced

2 sticks of celery, diced

3 tomatoes, peeled, seeded and chopped

2 tablespoons olive oil

80ml Cognac

350ml dry white wine or 235ml dry white
   vermouth

2 tablespoons chopped tarragon

1 bay leaf

1 garlic clove, peeled and crushed with the
   side of a knife

a pinch of cayenne pepper

50g long-grain rice

450ml fish stock

450ml chicken stock

240ml double cream

salt and black pepper

2–3 tablespoons finely chopped chervil and
   tarragon, to serve

DIRECTIONS

Fill a large pot with 5cm of cold water and 2 teaspoons of salt. Bring to the boil and add the lobsters. Cover with a tight-fitting lid and return to the boil, then lower the heat and cook for around 12 minutes, until bright red. Remove the lobsters and keep the cooking liquid to one side. Split the lobsters in half lengthways. Remove and discard the sac from the head and the intestine that runs along the

back. If there is any coral, remove this and reserve. Remove the meat from the claws and tails and refrigerate along with the coral. Keep the shells and legs to one side.

Melt 40g of butter in a heavy saucepan, add the carrot, onion and celery and cook gently for about 8 minutes until the vegetables are tender and the onions are translucent; they should not brown. Add the tomatoes, cook for a further 3 minutes and set aside. This is the mirepoix.

Pour the olive oil in the bottom of a casserole and set over a moderate heat. When the oil is hot but not smoking, add the lobster shell and legs. Do not overcrowd the pan; sauté in batches if necessary. Turn frequently and cook for 4–5 minutes until the shells are deep red. This will give the soup its colour. Once sautéed, lower the heat and season with salt and pepper. Pour on the Cognac, ignite and shake the casserole vigorously. When the flames have died down, pour on the wine or vermouth. Add the tarragon, bay leaf, mirepoix, garlic and cayenne pepper, then cover the casserole and simmer for 20 minutes.

Remove the lobster pieces and extract any remaining meat, transferring it to the bowl in the fridge. Chop the shells and set aside in another bowl. Purée the cooking sauce in a blender or food processor, pass through a sieve, then return to the blender. Do not wash the casserole.

Rinse the rice. Bring the fish stock, chicken stock and 250ml of the reserved lobster cooking liquid to the boil in a large pan, add the rice and bring back to the boil. Lower the heat and simmer, covered, for 20 minutes. Drain the rice, reserving the cooking liquid.

Add the rice and half of the reserved lobster meat to the blender containing the puréed cooking sauce and blend again using some of the cooking water from the rice to loosen the mixture. Remove from the blender and set aside.

Heat 85g of butter in the casserole. Once bubbling, add the lobster shells and legs and sauté for 2–3 minutes to heat thoroughly. Scrape the contents of the casserole into the blender and purée, flicking the blender on and off. Sieve the purée into a bowl, using a wooden spoon to extract as much butter as possible. Scrape the underside of the sieve with a rubber spatula to ensure that you have all the butter. Set this lobster butter aside.

Heat 30g of the lobster butter in a frying pan until bubbling, then add the remaining lobster meat and season lightly with salt and pepper. Sauté for 2 minutes over a moderate heat, then add a splash of Cognac or dry white vermouth and cook until the liquid has evaporated. Put the lobster meat into the unwashed casserole with the previously prepared soup mixture. Bring the bisque to a simmer just before serving. It should be thick – if it needs thinning, add a little of the reserved rice cooking liquid. Season with cayenne pepper, salt and black pepper to taste. Just before serving, stir in the cream, remove from the heat and stir in the remaining lobster butter. Pour the bisque into a hot tureen and decorate with the chervil and tarragon. Serve with croûtons or Melba toast.

ORANGE JELLY

INGREDIENTS

2 calves' feet, large upper bone removed

3 litres water

200g sugar

juice of 1 orange and 1 lemon, with 6 strips
    of peel from both, sliced thinly to avoid
    the pith

2 egg whites

160ml dry white wine

a pinch of ground cinnamon

830ml freshly squeezed orange juice

DIRECTIONS

Soak the feet in cold water for 2–3 hours.
Drain the feet and put them in a pot, covering
with fresh cold water. Bring to the boil and
simmer for 10 minutes. Drain, rinse well,
return them to the pot and cover with the
3 litres of water. Bring to the boil, cover, lower
the heat to barely simmering point and cook
at this temperature for 7 hours. During the
cooking process, skim the fat from the surface
every hour. At the end of cooking, skim off
all the fat. Sieve the liquid and leave to cool.
When cold, remove any remaining fat with
a spoon at first, then with a cloth dampened
with hot water. This should result in around
950ml of jelly.

Combine the sugar, the orange and lemon
juices and their peels in a saucepan and add
the jelly. Bring to the boil, take off the heat
and leave to cool for 10 minutes.

Beat the egg whites and white wine with a
pinch of cinnamon. Add this mixture to the
jelly, and bring back to the boil while whisking.
Simmer for 15 minutes, whisking occasionally.
Line a sieve with muslin and pass the jelly
through, then set aside until nearly cold.

Let the freshly squeezed orange juice settle
for half an hour after squeezing, then pass it
through a muslin cloth. Stir it into the jelly.
Pour into a mould and chill for at least 4 hours.
To unmould, dip the mould into hot water for
a second, wipe dry and turn out onto a serving
dish or platter.

LULU COX

Ecological Land Cooperative
United Kingdom

William Scott, *Still Life (Yellow Table)*
Oil on canvas, 72 x 92 cm. © Estate of William Scott 2021

The name of this dish derives from the Scotsman's version of roast woodcock, which is traditionally served on a slice of toast. Instead of the woodcock, we have anchovy paste and scrambled eggs. If you don't have the luxury of your own chickens, we implore you to buy the most naturally raised eggs you can. Chickens, as livestock, play a vital role in an ecological farming system. The more diverse their diet, the more delicious and thus nutritious the eggs will be.

Anchovy paste is a thick, glossy and perfectly smooth-textured creation. The more anchovy paste you make in a batch, the easier this is to achieve. I don't advise halving this recipe. It works best made in a blender, but if you just have a Nutribullet, it is also achievable with a little practice and perseverance. This anchovy paste is also delicious without the egg on top, or can be served with raw crudités. Any leftovers can be stored in the fridge for up to three days.

Do not be afraid of cooking, as your ingredients will know, and misbehave. — Fergus Henderson

SCOTCH WOODCOCK

INGREDIENTS

100g tinned anchovies
1 garlic clove, grated
1 tablespoon red wine vinegar
300ml olive oil
a knob of unsalted butter
9 eggs, beaten
4 slices of bread
salt and black pepper

DIRECTIONS

Place the anchovies, garlic and red wine vinegar into the small bowl of your blender with a splash of cold water. Blitz until you have a thick paste. You may need to add a little more water, but go gently as you don't want it to become too loose – it shouldn't be runny.

Once you have the desired consistency, slowly start to trickle in the olive oil until you have the consistency of mayonnaise. If it's too thick, loosen with water as this means it's on the brink of splitting. Imagine you're forcing two ingredients together (the oil and anchovies). They don't want to bond but with careful persuasion they will, and the result is magic. Season with black pepper.

To scramble the eggs, place the butter in a heavy based pan over a low heat. Allow the butter to melt and start to foam in the base of your pan before pouring in the eggs and seasoning with salt and a liberal grind of black pepper. Every few minutes, agitate the base of the pan with a wooden spoon – this gentle technique produces large, soft pillows of egg rather than small pieces.

Toast the bread, spread with butter (if you feel the urge), then spread with your anchovy paste. Finally add a hearty pile of omega-rich, bright yellow delicious eggs. Serves 4.

AGNES AND JACK DAVISON

The Trussell Trust
United Kingdom

Illustration by C.W. Smallbones, 2021

CARAMEL, PINE NUT & SESAME ICE CREAM

Don't forget to put the freezer bowl from your ice cream maker in the freezer at least 2 hours before you want to make your ice cream.

INGREDIENTS
285ml double cream
300ml full-fat milk
115g golden caster sugar
1 vanilla pod
3 large free-range egg yolks
1 tablespoon black sesame seeds
a handful of pine nuts

CARAMEL
200g sugar
85g unsalted butter at room temperature
120ml double cream
1 teaspoon sea salt

DIRECTIONS
Firstly, make the custard. Pour the cream and milk into a heavy based pan, along with half the sugar. Split the vanilla pod in half lengthways, scoop out the seeds, then add the seeds and pod to the pan. Heat over a low heat, stirring occasionally, until steaming but not boiling. Remove from the heat and set aside for 30 minutes.

While the vanilla is infusing, make the caramel. Place the sugar in a heavy based pan over a medium-low heat until it has completely melted, swirling the pan gently every 20 seconds or so and keeping an eye on the mixture as it clumps together and then melts. Once melted, remove from the heat immediately and stir in the butter, which will bubble up; keep stirring. Finally add the cream and salt and stir until combined. Set aside.

Coming back to the custard, put the egg yolks into a small bowl with the remaining sugar and beat until the mixture falls in thick ribbons. Add about 125ml of the cooled vanilla milk mixture and beat into the egg yolks to slacken them.

Remove the vanilla pod and reheat the milk until it just comes to the boil, then remove from the heat and stir the egg yolk mixture into the pan. Return the pan over a low heat and stir for 8–10 minutes until the custard coats the back of the spoon, watching that it doesn't boil. Pour the custard into a heatproof bowl, then place into a larger bowl of iced water and leave to cool for a minimum of 20 minutes – the custard should be very cold before adding to the ice cream machine.

With the machine running, pour in the cold custard and churn as long as your machine requires. While churning, toast the sesame seeds and pine nuts in a dry pan. Once it resembles very soft serve ice cream, stir in the caramel and nuts, place into a freezer container and freeze for a minimum of 2 hours. Remove from the freezer 15 minutes before serving.

GINEVRA ELKANN

Sosteniamoci
Milan and Rome, Italy

Ginevra Elkann photographed by Giacomo Gaetani, 2021

During lockdown, I discovered the joys of home schooling – not my talent. So after a bout of hysteria, I would take refuge in the kitchen, open recipe books and discover real cooking. And also cooking with all its appliances – egg beater, food processor, oven, freezer, fridge, all became my best friends. The only one I never managed to be at peace with is the dishwasher. I prefer washing the dishes by hand than loading the machine. I don't know why – maybe because it also means having to unload it.

Italians use a lot of Parmesan in their cuisine – on pasta, on rice, in soup, in mashed potatoes, in meatballs, basically everywhere. Yes, some people hate it, say it smells like sick. But to us Italians it's almost like salt. An essential ingredient. You need to grate a huge chunk almost every day. I used to do it clumsily with an old-fashioned grater. After a few minutes, my arm started to hurt and my hands slowly entered arthritis mode and I realised I was only half way through. So you can imagine my joy when I understood I could just cut the Parmesan in chunks, put it in the food blender and it would do the work in under a minute.

My favourite discovery was this recipe, given to me by my friend Osanna, who is a mother of four and an excellent cook. It is perfect for summer, very easy to make and delicious. It's all about good ingredients and the food processor.

RISO ALLA CRUDAIOLA

You will need about 10 cherry tomatoes, 5 basil leaves, 2 tablespoons of olive oil, salt and 2 tablespoons of grated Parmesan cheese. You can also use a clove of garlic if you like it, or some almonds. You put all the ingredients in a food processor and grind them until they are all cut in very small pieces. The mixture should look like a red pesto sauce. In the meantime, boil some rice, any kind will work here. When it's ready, let the rice cool a little and then pour the sauce on it and mix well to combine. Et Voilà! It's extremely easy and delicious. This sauce also works very well on pasta.

TIN GAO

Ou nǐ hé xiáng
Lotus Farm near Beijing, China

This recipe is a lazy way to cook chicken legs in a rice cooker and is just for inspiration – please be more creative than me and add other ingredients!

If you want to cook rice to go with your chicken, there are two ways. You can cook the rice on its own in your rice cooker after you have cooked the chicken, flavouring it with chicken oil, or you can cook the rice at the same time as the chicken. Add the rice first to the rice cooker with a bit of water, then put it on to cook in the normal way. Half way through cooking, add the chicken and other ingredients and continue to cook until the rice and chicken are done.

RICE COOKER SALTED CHICKEN LEGS

INGREDIENTS
3 chicken drumsticks
2 teaspoons salt
1 garlic clove, sliced
2 spring onions, shredded
3 dried red chillies
5 small slices of ginger

SAUCE
3 tablespoons light soy sauce
1 tablespoon dark soy sauce
½ teaspoon sugar
1 tablespoon Chinese cooking rice wine

OPTIONAL EXTRAS
⅓ teaspoon black or white pepper
sprinkle of white sesame seeds
½ teaspoon oyster soy sauce
⅓ teaspoon sesame oil

DIRECTIONS
Massage the chicken legs with the salt and set aside for at least 5 minutes. Place in the rice cooker skin side down (to crisp up the skin), then add the garlic, spring onions, dried chillies and ginger.

Pour over the sauce ingredients and any of the optional extras you like, set the rice cooker to Rice mode and after 25-40 minutes (depending on your machine) it will be done. Serves 1 with rice.

RAMA GHEERAWO

The Akshaya Patra Foundation
India and United Kingdom

Foundational Values, 2021

On 10 February 2021, the Helen Hamlyn Centre for Design and the Royal College of Art held the first meeting of the Creative Leaders Circle. Over 100 people from around 30 countries attended to cook up new ideas about leadership. Most of what we have been taught about leadership is wrong, so the circle brought together three types of people to hear and share: established leaders, emerging leaders and - the biggest group of all - people who were never billed to be leaders. Many of us, including myself, are in the last group.

What people wanted was NOT the following, all of which make 21st-century leadership taste wrong:
— An ego broadcasting from a podium
— The tallest or loudest person in the room
— People who act one way at work and hold a different set of values at home
— Leadership that is survival of the fittest
— Wearing a blue shirt, and accessorising with a firm handshake

What was brought to the table was:
— The wisdom and heartfelt action of the empath
— Leadership as personal and professional Clarity
— Creativity celebrated as an attribute, not as a dream-edged wish
— Leadership that personally develops, and universally applies
— Wearing Authenticity, and accessorizing with Trust

New dishes are sometimes the result of the right circumstance. Together, we reframed the menu of leadership and worked up an appetite to truly democratize ideas. I leave you with a thought that materialized, one which is true for both lunch and leadership - it is not enough to be invited to the table. You also have to eat. We will be sharing the results shortly and invite you to partake.

MOLLY GODDARD

North Paddington Food Bank
London, United Kingdom

A QUICK AND VERY EASY
FISH LUNCH

We served this smoked mackerel paté with spelt bread that Tom Travis left on my doorstep, and Tom Shickle's pickled red cabbage, which he made with vinegar and bay leaves. Cold white wine is essential for a sunny lunch.

INGREDIENTS

3–4 smoked mackerel fillets

a dash of olive oil

1–2 tablespoons Greek yoghurt

about 1 tablespoon Dijon mustard

butter

½ lemon

salt and pepper

toast, to serve

DIRECTIONS

Remove the flesh from the mackerel fillets and place in a bowl. Take the mackerel skins and fry for a couple of minutes in a tiny bit of olive oil until crispy, then drain on kitchen paper. Flake the flesh using two forks, then add a dollop of yoghurt – start with a tablespoon and add more if needed. I like to add a large dollop of mustard – but you can use a bit less – and lots of salt and pepper. Mix it all together with a fork. Lightly toast the bread and spread well with lots of butter. Place the mackerel on the toast and sprinkle with a little lemon juice. I like to pile it high. Top with the crispy mackerel skin.

LAILA GOHAR

ROAR New York
New York City, United States

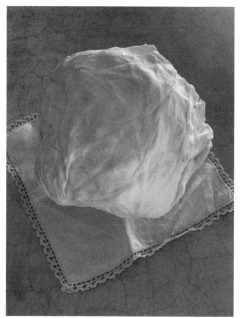

SAUERKRAUT

Learn to preserve. The only tools necessary are your hands and nose. Cabbage is a good start. Chop a head of cabbage into ribbons and place in a large bowl. Add about 1½ tablespoons of salt. I also grate in a little fresh turmeric and a jalapeño if I have them. Massage with your hands. If you added turmeric, then use a glove or else you'll dye your fingers yellow, like me. You'll notice that after a few minutes the cabbage will reduce in volume by about half. Find a large jar and make sure it's clean and dry. Pack the cabbage in with its liquid and pack down as you go along. You want all the cabbage to be submerged, so find a smaller item (I used a glass) to weight it down and place on top of the cabbage then close the jar. Keep it in a cool dry place to ferment for at least 3 days. There are no rules for when sauerkraut is 'done'. Start smelling and tasting it after 3 days, and when it tastes good to you, move the jar to the fridge. Sauerkraut keeps in the fridge for a long time. It will definitely outlive corona.

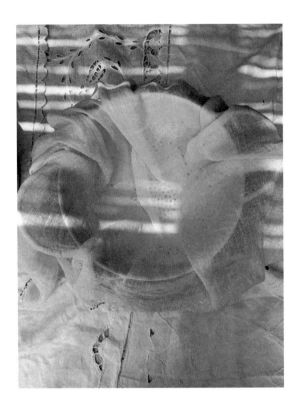

RICOTTA

If you have milk, you can make ricotta. Bring a big heavy based pan of milk with a tiny bit of salt to a simmer over a low heat. About 2 litres of milk will yield 250g of ricotta. Heating the milk should take a while. Maybe half an hour. Bring to the point just before boiling. There should be tiny bubbles and steam but not a rolling boil. Take off the heat and, for 2 litres of milk, add 4 tablespoons of vinegar. Mix gently a couple of times with a wooden spoon. You'll see that the milk will curdle right away, separating the curds and whey. Let the milk sit undisturbed for a little while, then line a colander with a cheesecloth (any clean gauzy fabric will do) and put that over a bowl. Remove the big curds using a slotted spoon and place in the cheesecloth, and then gently pour over the rest. The whey (liquid) can be reserved for baking or adding to smoothies if you want extra protein. Hang the cheesecloth to drip over the sink or from a tree. I like to eat the ricotta still warm with lots of honey and some black pepper.

CANDIED ORANGE

As a kid I didn't like candied orange. I guess it's one of those things, like coffee or anchovies, that you learn to appreciate with age.

Peel the skins from a few oranges. Now line the orange peel up and cut it into long strips of equal size. Bring a pot of water to the boil and boil the orange strips for a few minutes, then remove and put in iced water. Repeat this step with fresh water. This is to remove the bitterness from the pith. Meanwhile, make a simple syrup. This is a 1:1 ratio of sugar and water: 1 cup of sugar and 1 cup of water. I put camomile flowers in mine because I had them, but this is not essential. Mine made me feel good, though. Bring the syrup to the boil, then add the orange strips and simmer on low, covered, for an hour. Remove the candied orange and lay the pieces out to dry. This will take a while, maybe a night. You can stop there, or melt some dark chocolate and dip the orange into it and then leave to harden.

PHOEBE GREENWOOD

Shelter from the Storm
London, United Kingdom

This is a leftovers Lockdown Luncheon. We have a toddler, so all dishes are repurposed for days. Today it's baked potato with hummus (thank you to the amazing Oli Food Centre on the Walworth Road) and Elizabeth David's aubergine parmigiana, cooked with added beetroot. Our new lunch normal seems to be eating lots of clotted cream and scones, something I've not eaten since I was a kid. My Dad was from Devon. On holidays there we would visit nearby farms to buy polystyrene cups filled with the heavenly stuff. The scones are my Aunt Sarah's recipe.

This meal is really just an excuse to eat off my dad's collection of Ann Stokes pottery. It's why beetroot gets added to almost everything – the colours look so heavenly. It's like eating off a Bonnard. Ann was a fabulous artist with a twinkle that could power the national grid. Her annual Christmas sale at her home studio in Hampstead was fuelled by mulled wine and the bohemian spirit of her St Ives 'education' among the Ben Nicholson set. She loved the natural world with the passion and knowledge of a zoologist. Our son is now learning about spiny dogfish, thanks to Ann's plates. Her first rhinoceros, made as a soup tureen, was for the historian Ernst Gombrich. We've got an ingenious holder just for weeds and wild flowers. My father, a gallerist and curator, included Ann in a group show at the Hayward. It ruffled feathers (Ann loved birds and we have gorgeous, bird of prey dishes with soaring wings) because he dared to show a 'potter' alongside artists such as Gilbert and George. While we can't see any family in lockdown, it's comforting to think of my Dad's partner Francois also eating off his 'Ann' plates. And the larger extended family of fans. Ann was much loved and collected.

WHOLEMEAL YOGHURT SCONES

INGREDIENTS
450g wholemeal plain flour
1 teaspoon baking powder
50g sugar
125g sultanas
75g butter
225ml natural yoghurt

DIRECTIONS
Sieve the flour into a mixing bowl and combine with the baking powder, sugar and sultanas. Rub in the butter with your fingertips and bind with the yoghurt to make a dough. Press out on a floured surface and cut into rounds. Place on a baking sheet, brush the tops with yoghurt and bake until golden.

ESTELLE HANANIA

Potager! Liberté!
Les Lilas, France

La découverte (The Discovery), 2020

Pommes (Apples), 2020

En cuisine
(In the kitchen), 2020

AMANDA HARLECH

Shrewsbury Food Bank
Shrewsbury, United Kingdom

Photographs by Tallulah Harlech, 2020

Lockdown means invention and experimentation with what you have to hand. Purple sprouting broccoli, chard, onions, celery and kale, cabbage and leaf beet are all in season now. This is a great recipe for vegetable broth into which you can chuck any vegetables, except aubergines, potatoes or tomatoes (members of the nightshade family). Organic miso paste is delicious and a fantastic healer and protector.

VEGETABLE BROTH

INGREDIENTS
1 litre water
2 sachets of dashi stock
2 dessertspoons organic miso paste

CHOICE OF VEGETABLES
cabbage, finely sliced
kale, sliced with stalks removed
chard, sliced with stalks separated
pak choy
bok choy
celery, finely chopped
spring onions, shredded
leeks, finely sliced
spinach
broccoli, cut into florets
cauliflower, cut into florets
purple sprouting broccoli
green beans
carrots, thinly sliced
beetroot, thinly sliced
beet tops
garlic, sliced
ginger, sliced
onion, sliced
parsley and chives

DIRECTIONS
It's very, very simple. While the water comes to the boil in a big pan, prepare all the vegetables you are using. Add the dashi stock. When the stock begins to simmer, add onions, leeks, celery, chard stalks, carrots or beetroot and cook for about 7 minutes until tender.

Next add the green leafy vegetables and simmer for about 5 minutes, stirring from time to time so everything cooks evenly. Remove the pan from the heat and let it stand for a minute, then stir in the miso paste. I use chopsticks with the spoon submerged in the broth to mix in the miso paste. And there you are! Done.

Serve with rice, blanched chard with garlic and olive oil, a huge salad. A glass of burgundy. And you can have any leftovers for breakfast the next day with a poached egg.

MARGOT HENDERSON

Magic Breakfast
United Kingdom

Fergus Henderson eating Margot's celeriac soup,
photograph by Oliver Harty, 2021

Celeriac is a glorious vegetable, an old-fashioned all-rounder that loves to soak up everything around it. This great bulbous, beautiful vegetable, like some incredible sculpture, can be treated like a potato but with added bonuses. It is structurally brilliant, holding itself well, it's happy raw and loves to be made into broths, stews, mashes. Add to stocks; fish and meat alike enjoy its company. Somehow it loves you and soothes. A great vegetable to have any time of the year. This is one of my all-time favourite soothing soups, a bowl of goodness which warms and caresses. It's as gentle on the eye as the stomach.

CELERIAC SOUP

INGREDIENTS
70ml extra virgin olive oil
1 onion, sliced
2 garlic cloves, sliced
1 large celeriac
1.5 litres Dashi Stock (see below)
2 tablespoons white miso paste
salt and pepper

DIRECTIONS
Heat the oil in a large pot and cook the onion and garlic gently with the lid on until tender. You are looking for a white soup, so try not to brown them too much.

Meanwhile, peel the celeriac using a bread knife or a large sharp knife. Carefully take away the outer skin, then slice the flesh into even pieces, about 3cm by 2cm. Then add to the pot with your onions, stir, replace the lid and cook at a gentle heat. Let them get to know each other.

Pour in just enough dashi stock to cover the celeriac, add a pinch of salt and simmer until the celeriac is cooked through. Purée the celeriac and liquid with the miso until the soup is smooth. I use a Nutribullet to do my liquidizing, but any sort of mushing equipment will work, even a mouli. Check and adjust the seasoning – the miso does bring salt, so check carefully. Serves 4.

DASHI STOCK

The new love of my life, this is vegan dashi but it can also be made with bonito flakes. The taste is heavenly. The piece of seaweed is a wonderful thing, bringing a simple, uncomplicated flavour to dishes.

INGREDIENTS
10cm piece of kombo
3 dried shiitaki mushrooms
1.5 litres water

DIRECTIONS
In a pot, bring the kombu, shiitaki and water to the boil, then reduce the heat and simmer for 1 hour. It will appear frothy on the top. Drain and allow to cool. Dashi will keep in the fridge for a few days.

KATERINA JEBB

Meals on Wheels
Paris, France

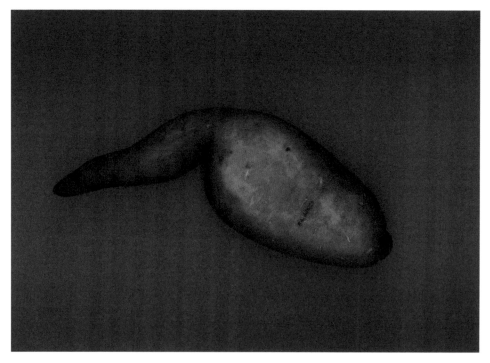

Sweet Potato, Rome, 2018

Cross-stitch by Julia Stuhler for Poot It In Yer Bag, 2021
Read more about the Poot It In Yer Bag project on page 32.

YOLANDA JIMENEZ

The Okra Project
United States

It's very warm in Mexico City at the moment and I want to have something refreshing and fun and Mexican, something you could enjoy from lunchtime till late at night, with a strong taste of lime (we like to put lime in everything). The sweetness of the coconut and rosemary add a nice balance and this reminds me of the classic Mexican beach cocktails.

ROSEMARY'S HONEY BABY

INGREDIENTS
45ml Yola Mezcal
15ml coconut cream
15ml lime juice
7.5ml Dolin Blanc
15ml Rosemary Honey Syrup (see below)

DIRECTIONS
Pour all the ingredients over ice and stir vigorously, or shake in a cocktail shaker, strain into a glass and serve. Add fresh or charred rosemary to decorate.

ROSEMARY HONEY SYRUP

Place 125ml of water and 125ml of honey in a saucepan over a medium heat and stir for 2–3 minutes, or until the honey has completely dissolved. Bring to the boil, then reduce the heat to low, add about 15g of chopped rosemary and cook, uncovered, for 30 minutes, stirring occasionally. Remove from the heat and pour into a jar through a fine mesh strainer. It'll store perfectly in the refrigerator if you don't finish it all.

REBECCA MAY JOHNSON

FareShare
United Kingdom

Clouds gathered as I cooked this aubergine pasta dish in a small wooden sailing boat on the River Stour between Essex and Suffolk. A storm had not been forecast, just a little rain. As we ate the rich and savoury pasta, we did not expect that a turn in the weather would put us in a life-threatening situation. But not long after lying down our heads to sleep, the boat began lurching up and down and the little tender attached to the stern on a rope began smashing into the side. I went up to have a look and found the water transformed into a big sea, with waves several metres high.

Our anchor had ripped from the bottom and we were drifting into the channel used by cargo boats. It was pitch black with no moon. After a few moments of panic, I turned on the engine and steered us over the rolling waves in the dark, keeping a close eye on the electronic charts to avoid running aground or hitting rocks. We navigated up the river until we eventually found a mooring to tie up to and wait out the storm overnight.

Perhaps eating this dish gave me the strength to take us out of the storm and navigate to safety.

AUBERGINE PASTA FOR A STORM

INGREDIENTS

6 tablespoons good olive oil
1 aubergine, cut into 2cm dice
6 anchovy fillets
2 garlic cloves, finely sliced
a pinch of dried chilli flakes
1 tin of tomatoes in their juice
200g pasta
salt

DIRECTIONS

Heat the olive oil in a deep frying pan until hot and fry the aubergine pieces in small batches until soft. When each little batch is cooked, remove to a plate lined with kitchen paper.

Add another tablespoon of oil to the pan if necessary, then turn the heat right down and add the anchovies and garlic. Stir to break up the anchovies so that they are disintegrating. Add the chilli flakes, then the tinned tomatoes. Cook on a low heat for 10 minutes, breaking up the tomatoes with your wooden spoon. Then add the aubergines and cook for a further 10 minutes on a low heat. Check for seasoning, adding additional salt if desired. Allow to rest while you cook the pasta.

Boil a pot of water in which to cook the pasta then add a tablespoon of salt. Cook the pasta until it is tender with a little bite left. Toss the pasta in the pan with the aubergine and serve. A glass of red wine, some bread and a green salad go nicely.

IBRAHIM KAMARA

Hackney Food Bank
London, United Kingdom

All images by Ibrahim Kamara, 2020

EDWARD KAY

Dads House
United Kingdom

Pickles, 2020
Photographs by Jonathan Bassett

Pickles, 2020

MICHÈLE LAMY
& RICK OWENS

Oko Farms
New York City, United States

Michèle Lamy filmed by Rick Owens, Paris, 2020

Michèle Lamy has made lunch for herself and Rick Owens on the terrace outside their house in Paris in April 2020 during the first lockdown. The sun is shining. The food is beautifully laid out on the table; Rick asks Michèle to describe what she has made.

RICK: Okay, well, there are scallops, how were the scallops prepared?

MICHÈLE: So the scallops today are with salad – they are grilled, they are over a *mâche* [lamb's lettuce] and egg salad. But I know this way you are not going to eat them….this is just for the pictures.

RICK *(laughing)*: Oh because I'm not going to have a salad.

MICHÈLE: Because you don't eat salad…you are missing a lot, but anyway you can have a few bits. And then you are going to eat it with those fabulous onion and potatoes, that the Swiss would call rösti. And then we have our usual of the season, some great melon – in fact these melons come from Morocco, they are not in season in France. And then we have the avocado, and *La mangue* that we usually call papaya but it is a mango.

RICK: Whaat?

MICHÈLE: Yes! *(laughing)*

RICK: Are you kidding me?

MICHÈLE: *À table s'il vous plait*, I'm hungry! And a sauce vinaigrette, with a little bit of balsamic from Modena.

RICK: Well honey, that looks delicious.

MICHÈLE *(laughing and smoking)*: Yes! So I'm having a little aperitif in the sun, and I'm very hungry so come to the table.

JEREMY LEE

DeliverAid and The Food Chain
London, United Kingdom

The realm of the omelette, or kudu, or frittata or tortilla or quiche, is one of boundless choice. Eggs take remarkable pleasure in teaming up with all manner of produce – in this instance, sprouting broccoli, leaves too please, and cheese. I used crème fraîche, for that was in the fridge, but cream is delicious also. Bacon, of course, is entirely at the cook's discretion but I am an addict and cannot do without. This recipe will happily feed two, or just one, warm from the oven and cold the next day, a great fridge favourite.

AN OMELETTE OF SORTS

INGREDIENTS

4 rashers of streaky bacon (I like smoked)
1 soupspoon olive oil
a small handful of sprouting broccoli
4 eggs
a small tub of crème fraîche or cream
a small posy of flat-leaf parsley, chopped
3 tablespoons grated cheese (I used Lancashire
   and a heel of Montgomery's Cheddar)
a pinch of dried savoury or thyme
salt and pepper

DIRECTIONS

Heat the oven to 200°C. Cut the bacon into small strips and fry lightly in the olive oil in a cast iron pan. Slice the broccoli and boil until tender. Drain. Beat the eggs and add the crème fraîche, then all the other ingredients, including the broccoli. Season with salt and pepper. Tip the mixture over the bacon in the warm pan. Mix well and place in the oven. Reduce the heat to 180°C and bake for 25 minutes or so until just set. Let sit for 5 minutes then eat warm with salad, bread and butter, of course.

SUPRIYA LELE

The Felix Project
London, United Kingdom

I'm in lockdown in my flat in London and homesick for my mum's cooking, which is always a source of comfort in tough times. She has a very busy schedule as a consultant doctor in the NHS, yet she always has time to put these dishes together, so I decided to make her tadka daal and baingan bharta (a roasted aubergine mash) – very simple and humble traditional Indian food. I think she would say I'm just about mastering these recipes of hers! I roasted some baby new potatoes in turmeric and cumin to accompany, and served with quickly pickled onions, peanut chutney and a cucumber raita. Not to forget an ice-cold beer.

TADKA DAAL

INGREDIENTS

200g daal (I use toor daal, but you can use any daal/lentils)
1–1.5 litres water
1 tablespoon ground turmeric
1 dried red chilli (optional)
salt

FOR THE TADKA

ghee, butter or oil
½ teaspoon mustard seeds
½ teaspoon cumin seeds
½ onion, finely chopped
1–2 garlic cloves, chopped
a thumb-sized piece of ginger, grated or finely chopped
fresh chilli, chopped, to taste
a pinch of chilli powder
½ fresh tomato, chopped
fresh coriander, finely chopped, to garnish

DIRECTIONS

I cook my lentils in a pressure cooker, which saves time; however, here's how you do it without. Soak your lentils in water for an hour or so, then rinse. Place in a saucepan with the water, the turmeric and a little salt. I like to put a dried red chilli in at this point to add some warmth during the cooking process. Bring to the boil and simmer for around an hour, stirring occasionally so that the daal doesn't catch on the bottom of the pan. It's not an exact science, so just top up with water if you feel you need more. You'll know when the daal is cooked through, when you can mash it easily with the back of a spoon and the lentils break down and go creamy. I like to have mine at a medium consistency, so I always add a bit of water at the end of cooking to thin it out a bit. You can also put fresh spinach or any other greens in towards the end. Taste for salt, and add some extra if you need.

To make the tadka, heat some ghee, butter or oil in another saucepan over a high heat and add your mustard and cumin seeds. Reduce the heat to medium and wait for the mustard seeds to begin to pop and the cumin seeds to become aromatic. Add the onion, garlic, ginger and fresh chilli and fry for a couple of minutes. Indian food is all about cooking in stages, so once these are starting to colour up nicely, add your chilli powder and your tomatoes. Cook for a further 2-3 minutes.

Traditionally, the daal is poured on top of the tadka, but for ease pour your tadka directly onto your daal and mix together. Garnish with finely chopped coriander.

BAINGAN BHARTA

You can cook your aubergines directly over a gas flame if you feel comfortable, until they blacken, deflate and char. But my mum makes her recipe using the oven. Either way, this is an amazingly simple and delicious dish that we would eat almost every week.

INGREDIENTS

2 aubergines

2-3 tomatoes

2 small onions, peeled and halved

oil

1 teaspoon mustard seeds

1 teaspoon cumin seeds

1 fresh chilli, roughly chopped

½ teaspoon ground turmeric

1 heaped teaspoon each of ground cumin, ground coriander, chilli powder

salt

DIRECTIONS

Preheat the oven to 180°C. Place the aubergines, tomatoes and onions in a roasting dish, drizzle with oil and slow roast for 1½–2 hours, depending on the size of your veg. Remove from the oven and leave to cool. Once cool to the touch, remove the skin from the aubergines and put the flesh in a bowl with the roasted tomatoes and onions. Mash together.

Heat some oil in a frying pan and add the mustard and cumin seeds. Once the mustard seeds begin to pop, add your chilli and fry for a minute or two, then add the ground turmeric. Fry this for a brief minute before adding the mashed vegetables to the pan, along with your cumin, coriander and chilli powder. Turn the heat down to low. Mix everything together and add salt to taste. Leave it to cook for 5 minutes, then remove from the heat and leave to rest. Garnish with finely chopped coriander.

TURMERIC & CUMIN ROAST POTATOES

INGREDIENTS
a good handful of baby potatoes
2 teaspoons ground turmeric
3 teaspoons ground cumin
1 teaspoon chilli powder
a drizzle of olive oil
sea salt and freshly ground black pepper

DIRECTIONS
Preheat the oven to 200°C. Chop the potatoes in half and mix with the spices and oil in an oven dish. Season with salt and pepper and roast in the oven for around 45 minutes.

KELSEY LU

Soul Fire Farm
Petersburg, New York, United States

Above, clockwise from top left: *Gerardo, Chef Jake, Chef Angela, Bebe*
Opposite, left to right: *Simon, Matt*

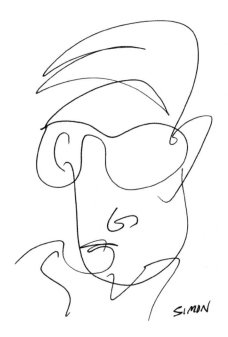

I came to Grand Cayman for a residency at Palm Heights before the lockdown began, to work on my album and various other projects. When things started to get serious, I made the decision to stay. I've created a studio in one of the suites and, since I don't have a full kitchen, I depend every day on the family meals prepared by the chefs of the hotel for the staff. It's the one time of the day when I get to see other people.

I've been fascinated with doing blind drawings of people for years. Blind drawing is when you look at someone and draw what you see instinctively, in seconds, without looking down at the paper. One of my favourite memories of doing them was after my show in Berlin. The show was such an emotionally charged experience that I decided to do a meet-and-greet at the merch table afterwards, where I'd do a blind drawing of each fan on the backs of my shirts. Looking into the eyes of a fan and making that connection with them for those seconds was so emotional. Many tears were shed and shared. For this Lockdown Luncheon, I decided to share blind drawings of the faces I've been sharing meals with over this lockdown. It's funny how unsettling it can be for the person being drawn. I suggest trying it, especially with strangers (at a safe distance, of course). Human connection is hope.

RICHARD MALONE

The Albert Kennedy Trust
United Kingdom

Lunch and paintings in the background by Richard Malone, 2020

I'm in lockdown in my flat in London, keeping myself busy constantly cooking and eating, in between drawing and catching up with my very best friends and family, as well as having brief drunken parties on Zoom. We've had an extended break from the studio since the last collection, and some upcoming sculpture shows of mine have been postponed. Usually at this time of year I'd get back home to Ardcavan in Wexford, and I'm definitely craving fresh air, beaches and home cooking. For my Lockdown Luncheon, I'm making a very traditional Irish meal, specific to where I'm from in Ireland (Co. Wexford) – rissoles, colcannon, cabbage and some Guinness soda bread on the side. I serve everything together with some red pepper relish. The meal is buttery, herby, fresh and indulgent and really extremely easy. It's filling, so I made it at around four o'clock, replacing lunch and dinnertime. As my grandmother said, 'Is maith an t-anlann an t-ocras' (Hunger is the best sauce).

Rissoles aren't super-popular in the rest of Ireland so have a really nostalgic connotation for me. They're very easy to make, and you can get delicious options all around Wexford. A lot of chippies make incredible versions – often from leftover chips or mashed potatoes. They are traditionally a working-class food made from leftovers and could be taken out fishing (Wexford is a fishing town). We think they came over from Europe via France or Norway. Both my grandad and my dad were working in factories when I was a child, and my mam in a local café, so after work on Fridays we'd often be in my grandmother's house with the rest of the grandchildren, and I remember getting to share breaded rissoles with some chips – it was very exciting. The food is incredible in this part of Ireland: local, fresh, unpretentious and affordable for everyone. We have the brilliant Kilmore seafood festival and the best fish in Ireland from the numerous quays, as well as having the Saltee Islands just off the coast.

I had my lunch with a nice rosé as the sun was shining. It reminds me of getting the train down to Rosslare from Wexford as a teenager with some cheap wine and stolen cigarettes for an all-night caravan party; very fond memories.

COLCANNON

Colcannon is incredibly easy and often made the day after having a meal of bacon and cabbage. I don't eat meat but was taught how to make colcannon by my grandmother Nellie and my mam Helen, using leftovers from the night before. You can have it on its own with parsley or with mustard sauce. My dad fries it for longer and lets the bottom crisp, which is delicious. To have with rissoles, I prefer it creamier, and serve it with fresh red cabbage.

INGREDIENTS

1 large onion, thinly sliced
rapeseed oil
3 garlic cloves, finely chopped
leftover boiled or mashed potatoes
butter
a few sprigs of thyme, chopped
leftover cooked cabbage
salt and pepper

DIRECTIONS

First I fry the onion in some rapeseed oil, adding the garlic after a few minutes. Next I mash the leftover potatoes with lots of butter, then add it to the onions with the chopped thyme and salt and pepper to taste. I cook it on medium heat – I don't want the crispy bottom for this one so I keep stirring. Finally I add my cabbage – I'm too lazy to chop it and use another board and knife so I just tear it into strips and add to the pan, stirring continuously until it's all mixed together. I then turn down the heat and most likely add another bit of butter – because why not? – then cover the pan and cook until it's hot.

RED CABBAGE

While the colcannon is keeping warm, I chop some red cabbage and add to a pan over medium heat with a splash of soy sauce, some chilli flakes and a sprinkle of warm paprika.

GUINNESS SODA BREAD

Guinness soda bread is the last of the four pillars of this feast of a lunch today, served on the side along with the rissoles, colcannon and cabbage. My mam makes soda bread every day and her mother did too – I'm not really sure you can be Irish if you can't make a soda bread. For mine I add Guinness as well as some treacle and dark honey, and for the crust I use porridge oats and some dark muscovado sugar which melts during baking. If you don't have buttermilk, I recommend some oat milk with a good squeeze of lemon. It's divine.

The next day you can slice any leftover soda bread and fry it on the griddle with a fried banana, and add some salted butter and crème fraîche (or double cream) for a fantastic and indulgent dessert, obviously accompanied by some Barry's tea or a hot whiskey with ginger and cloves.

ANTONIA MARSH

We Are Grow
London, United Kingdom

Pasta pesto has been in my embarrassingly limited culinary repertoire since I was a student. During lockdown, we've been foraging for wild garlic in our local area and this delicious wild garlic pesto is the result – it's so cheap and easy to make.

WILD GARLIC PESTO

In a food processor, blend 200g of wild garlic leaves with 100g of grated Parmesan cheese, 100g of toasted pine nuts, a good drizzle of olive oil, a squeeze of lemon juice, some salt and some pepper. Any kind of pasta works with this pesto, but spaghetti is my favourite because it's so slurpy. We got a bit overexcited with our foraging and have loads of pesto left over which we keep in a big jar in the fridge. It lasts for ages.

RHUBARB POLENTA CAKE

For our sweet and tangy rhubarb polenta cake, we dug out some rhubarb from the freezer (500g, washed and chopped) and roasted it in the oven for 30-40 minutes with 50g of caster sugar and 4 tablespoons of water. In a bowl, we mixed 125g of coarse polenta with 1 teaspoon of baking powder, 200g of plain flour and 150g of caster sugar, then rubbed in 150g of butter chunks and the zest of a small orange until the mixture resembled breadcrumbs.

In another bowl, we mixed an egg with 2-4 tablespoons of milk and added this liquid to the dry mixture to make a soft, slightly sticky dough. (Don't overmix!) We pressed two-thirds of the mixture into a buttered cake tin, pushing it a little up the sides. We placed the drained rhubarb on top, leaving a rim around the edge, then followed with the remaining mixture. Don't worry if it doesn't cover evenly, the rhubarb will ooze out if it wants to, which is divine. We scattered over 1 tablespoon of demerara sugar and baked the cake for 45-50 minutes at 180°C. We let it cool before eating with a dollop of plain yoghurt. Yum!

RONAN MCKENZIE

Migrateful
United Kingdom

Breakfast (above), *Lunch* (opposite: top) and *Supper* (opposite: bottom).
Photographs by Ronan Mckenzie, 2020

LUCIE AND
LUKE MEIER

Food for Soul
Moderna, Italy

Since we're in Milan, we thought we would share one of our favourite versions of risotto. We don't like to recreate dishes that we can easily find in Milanese restaurants, simply because they're done so well here, but also because we like to be a bit more experimental with flavours. This risotto features roasted vegetables, and you can use many varieties.

The risotto itself, before adding the roasted vegetable purée, can be lovely on its own or as a side dish. While risottos can be quite substantial, the presence of lemon juice and a good amount of herbs keeps this dish light and aromatic, which is perfect for the late spring or early autumn here in Italy. We hope you enjoy it and try many variations of your own.

ROASTED VEGETABLE RISOTTO

INGREDIENTS

3 carrots
½ squash
2 potatoes (or sweet potatoes)
olive oil
1 onion
3 garlic cloves
1 lemon
7 springs of thyme
about 1.6 litres vegetable stock
300g arborio rice
1 tablespoon curry powder
sea salt and freshly ground black pepper

DIRECTIONS

Peel the carrots, squash and potatoes and cut them into small pieces. Put them in a bowl with a tablespoon of olive oil, season with salt and pepper and toss well. Lay them on a baking sheet and roast at 220°C for about 30 minutes until they are soft and caramelized.

Chop the onion, mince the garlic and squeeze the lemon juice into a bowl. Pull the thyme leaves from the stems, and heat the stock.

When the vegetables are done, take them out of the oven and let cool for a few minutes. Warm a bit of oil in a heavy pot or casserole, add the onions and sauté until translucent. Add the thyme and garlic, season with a little salt and sauté for 2 more minutes. Add the rice, lemon juice and curry powder, and continue stirring until the liquid has been absorbed by the rice. Add 1.2 litres of stock and cover the pot. Let it simmer for 15 minutes.

Put the vegetables in a blender with the remaining stock and blend until smooth. Taste the rice to ensure a proper al dente texture. Add the vegetable purée to the risotto and stir until all the liquid has been absorbed. Enjoy with a crisp white wine. Serves 6–8.

NORIKO MIURA

Poot It In Yer Bag
London, United Kingdom

During lockdown, I am eating a lot of seaweed or whitebait with rice as I live by the sea and it is in season. But it is not photogenic and looks terrifying for most people in the UK. So I am sharing a recipe for a dish I would eat for comfort if I were locked down in London.

When I was working at Leila's in Shoreditch, chef Tim was cooking at the café. Like many chefs, he could be so grumpy in the kitchen but he was also funny, loving, the sweetest person I have ever met. I loved his food so much and never tired of it. At lunchtime, I would eat everything he offered and my portion was always enormous, but he never forgot to give me a small pudding. His food was simple, hearty and utterly delicious – he put a lot of effort and care into his food. He could whip up a legendary chickpea soup, cullen skink, frittata or one of his many Spanish dishes, as many people will remember. He showed me how to make aioli and anchovy dressing. He shared this recipe with me as it is so simple even I can do it at home. In memory of chef Tim Dillon.

CHORIZO SOUP

INGREDIENTS
6–8 potatoes, peeled and cut into chunks
1 bunch of turnips, peeled and halved
1 packet of chorizo sausages
a chunk of pancetta, chopped
1–2 garlic cloves
1–2 good sprigs of rosemary
a handful of chopped greens, like cavolo nero

DIRECTIONS
Put all the ingredients, except the greens, into a heavy based pan and cover with water. Cook until the potatoes and chorizo are cooked through, adding the chopped greens for the final minute of cooking. Chorizo gives such a beautiful flavour, there's no need to add any seasoning. Buon appetito. Serves 4.

STRAWBERRY SHORTBREAD

I don't have a proper recipe for the pudding I am afraid, but you bake a thin base of crispy shortbread using good French butter. When cool, spread with fatty double cream with lots of vanilla bean paste added, then top with fresh English strawberries. Cut up and serve.

LUCY KUMARA MOORE

Neighbourhood Bites
London, United Kingdom

When I think of black and white photography, I think of Araki's series 'Sentimental Journey', made during his honeymoon and featuring his wife Yoko Aoki; Sam Contis's 'Deep Springs' series (I launched the book a few years ago); the heavy contrast of the Japanese Provoke Era and the grey tones of Vanessa Winship and Mark Steinmetz. This Lockdown Luncheon is

what I'd make if, in a dream world, they came over for a visit. I've always loved black and white things to eat: liquorice, nigella seeds, nori seaweed, cheese covered in ash, imperial mints, rice pudding, cream, icing sugar. Squid ink tagliatelle is a particular favourite…here I served it with manchego and egg, followed by dark fruit, elderflower and crème fraîche. The plates are set on Claire de Rouen wrapping paper which I commissioned from artist Christian Flamm. Both recipes are very easy and quick to make as I have a four-month-old son, Cyrus, and find it hard to sequester more than 15 minutes straight in the kitchen.

SQUID INK TAGLIATELLE WITH MANCHEGO & EGG

While the tagliatelle cooks, soft boil an egg, chop some parsley and grate the palest Manchego you can find. Make sure the tagliatelle is al dente! Dress with butter (I'm in a butter not olive oil mood), salt and pepper, then cut the egg in half and lay on top of the tagliatelle. Cover with the chopped parsley and grated Manchego.

DARK FRUIT, ELDERFLOWER & CRÈME FRAÎCHE

For dessert, slice blueberries, figs and black-berries and lay them on top of a dollop of crème fraîche. I have an elderflower tree in the garden so I added a sprig of flowers.

REGINALD MOORE

Chattanooga Community Kitchen
Tennessee, United States

A GRANDMOTHER'S VEGETABLE SOUP

I come from a family of extraordinary cooks in the Southern tradition. People who have graciously prepared meals for friends and strangers. In fact, my uncle ran a highly regarded restaurant for many years, which is still talked about with great reverence. My father, an excellent baker of cakes and pies, will spend hours poring over his collection of cookbooks in search of new baking delights.

We have always been a family that comes together over a good meal and heated conversations about food in general and food preparation in particular; be it my Aunt Wilma's Sunday potato salad or my Aunt Iva's ability to out-grill anyone foolish enough to take up the challenge. It is true: a family that eats together, stays together.

Ask anyone in the family and they will tell you that they learned how to set an immaculate table for two or how to stretch a meager meal to feed the many from my grandmother Lillian. Every meal that she cooked for us was special and, now that she is gone, missed.

For me she would make the most delicious vegetable soup with tender beef tips and roughly chopped potatoes and carrots that she would let simmer most of the day. This wasn't a soup strictly designated for the winter months. No, we had this soup all year round. It was such a treat between us that she even bought us matching soup bowls in which to enjoy it.

It is the base of the soup that stumps us. For among her many other dishes, it cannot be replicated by memory, sheer will or good fortune. Believe me, we have all tried and failed. Since my grandmother was of that generation of women who, by talent alone, knew how and when to add a pinch of this or a sprig of that, she never wrote anything down. Our taste buds long for those recipes that were written in invisible ink.

I still have my soup bowl.

Collage by Shiv Lyons for Poot It In Yer Bag, 2021
Read more about the Poot It In Yer Bag project on page 32.

FREYA
E. MORRIS

Sisters Uncut
United Kingdom

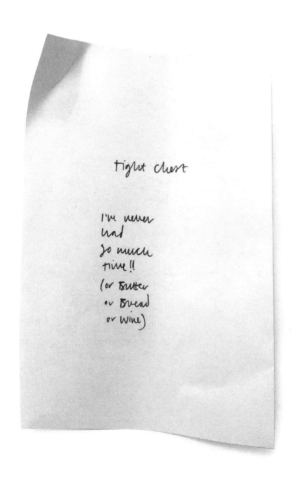

Tight Chest by Freya E. Morris, 2020

IAN PATTERSON

The Trussell Trust
United Kingdom

As I'm over 70, we haven't been to the shops for a while. I rummaged in the garden, the cupboards and the freezer – forgotten pastry! – and came up with the idea of making one of my favourites: pissaladière, with mostly wild salad leaves, followed by poached rhubarb. We ate it in the garden, to the accompaniment of the love calls of various small birds.

A POET'S LOCKDOWN LUNCH

INGREDIENTS

3 large onions
oil and butter
sprigs of thyme
a pinch of muscovado sugar
325g puff pastry
1 small tin of anchovy fillets
pitted black olives
green salad, to serve

DIRECTIONS

Slice the onions thinly and sweat them in a little oil and butter with some thyme leaves and a pinch of muscovado sugar. Let them cook down gently, on the lowest heat you can manage, for about an hour, giving them an encouraging stir from time to time. (It's important not to let them brown, let alone burn.) When they're done, take the puff pastry, roll out if necessary into a rectangle, and place it on a lightly floured baking sheet. Cut a border into the pastry all the way round, an inch from the edge, taking care not to cut right through: this will allow the edge of the tart to puff up round the filling. Now spread the onion evenly over the inner rectangle. Lay the anchovy fillets over it in a diamond pattern (I had to cut mine in half lengthways as I didn't have enough) and put an olive in each diamond. Stick it in a hot oven (200°C) for about 20 minutes, until crisp and golden. Serve with a green salad – I used Romaine lettuce, spiced up with dandelion leaves, garlic mustard (Jack-by-the-hedge) and sorrel from the garden.

POACHED RHUBARB

The rhubarb we followed it with (half of it from the garden) was poached in a glassful of white wine and a little demerara sugar in a medium oven for 15–20 minutes. After taking it out, I grated the zest of a blood orange over it, and left it to steep for a couple of hours.

JANINA PEDAN

Mercy Bakery
Yemen

Photograph by Romany Gilmour, 2020

This is a lunch that Charlie Gilmour and I made from foraged food around our family lockdown in West Sussex. Once you get into foraging, you will be surprised at how many things start turning up around you that are edible, even in urban areas. Soon it seems like everything is food and it is easy to end up in some sort of grey area where you start chewing random leaves. Be careful! There are poisonous things out there. We have been eating nettles non-stop for the past month and almost everyone is sick of them now, so we are looking forward to next season's menu. Here is our menu for now:

Nettle soup the Swedish way (with egg)
Nettle bread
Dandelion fritters
Wild garlic pesto
Wild leaf salad
Gorse & dandelion ice cream

STINGING NETTLE
"URTICA DIOICA"

NETTLE SOUP
THE SWEDISH WAY

NETTLE
BREAD

Fry some chopped onion in a little oil and add some chunks of potato. Add stock and let boil till the potatoes are cooked. Add the nettle tips and let boil for 5 minutes, or less, then season and blend the soup to the desired consistency. I like my nettle soup with a hard-boiled egg, the way one eats it in Sweden.

Pick LOADS of nettles, either tips or larger leaves – it doesn't matter too much as it will all get ground up. Dry the leaves in a very low oven or in the sun until dehydrated. Blitz in a coffee grinder into a fine powder. Use a basic white bread recipe and substitute some of the flour for nettle powder. You don't need loads. This is potent stuff.

WILD GARLIC
"ALLIUM URSINUM"

DANDELION FRITTERS

WILD GARLIC PESTO

Pick dandelion heads with some of the stem attached in the morning or at midday when the flowers are fully open (and less bitter). Dip them in a light batter and deep fry. Both leaves and flower heads can be used.

This pesto was made with a big proportion of roasted sunflower seeds, some Parmesan, olive oil and two handfuls of wild garlic leaves.

MUSTARD-GARLIC
"ALLIARIA PETIOLATA"

LADY'S SMOCK
"CARDAMINE PRATENSIS"

WATER MINT
"MENTHA AQUATICA"

WILD LEAF SALAD

We put every edible leaf we could find in this salad:

Wild water mint

Lady's smock

Dandelion leaf

Lime (linden) tree leaves and buds (everyone is crazy about the buds)

Garlic mustard

Wild lemon balm

GORSE & DANDELION ICE CREAM

Put some gorse and dandelion petals in a jug of milk and let steep overnight (only the yellow parts; avoid the green bit of the flower as it is bitter). Filter out the flowers and use the milk in a basic ice cream recipe. I added some condensed milk, which went well with the soft flavour of gorse. You can add some extra dandelion petals before freezing and when serving for a joyful yellow sprinkle.

LOLA PEPLOE

Les Restos du Coeur
France

Lola's grandmother Clotilde Peploe, Serifos, Greece, 1979

Lola's grandmother Clotilde Peploe, London, 1950

My grandmother learned to cook in her late fifties when she was living alone and painting on the remote Cycladic islands where supplies were few. She invented this dish and claimed it was a great delicacy. I think she lived off pretty much this and perhaps a few boiled eggs and a lump of goats' cheese here and there. Everyone in my family made fun of her but we all know her recipe by heart and when the cupboard is empty and someone's coming round for supper, we have all often used it – it can really do the trick, especially with a handful of fresh parsley and a cold glass of white wine. And it's a very, very cheap date.

RICE & CARAMELIZED ONIONS

Cook the rice until tender – any kind, brown or white (but the better quality the rice, the better the result). Fry some chopped onions in a little oil until caramelized, as many as possible as they reduce fast. Add a splash of fresh olive oil to the rice once drained, and salt and pepper to taste. At the last minute, pour on the onions. Soy or tamari can be drizzled on top for those who like it, and fresh parsley or coriander too.

PIGS: BOB, BARBARA AND BELINDA

Foodshare
United Kingdom

LUNCH FOR PIGS:
COOKED BY CHARLIE,
FRANK AND KATE BOXER &
EUGENIA SIMO GRIJALBO

Cook 5kg of macaroni until al dente, drain and place in a large pan or huge jelly mould. Pour over 3–4 litres of dissolved vegan jelly, any flavour – our guests very much enjoyed raspberry. Place a plate or chopping board on top of the pasta with a heavy weight on top and leave to set overnight.

Just before serving, turn out onto a huge plate or picnic blanket. Decorate with 4 litres of whipped cream. We coloured the cream pink to go with the jelly. Serves 3.

CHARLIE PORTER

Children with Voices
London, United Kingdom

This is today's take on the daily lunch that I've been eating on weekdays for 11 years now. The core ingredients are quinoa and smoked mackerel, accompanied by whatever in-season vegetables are available at Leila's Shop, Shoreditch, where I also get the mackerel and the kraut, which is by London Fermentary. The bowl is an A-Z West Container by Andrea Zittel, which can be ordered through her online store. The chair is by Marc Hundley and the dog is Orpheus, who will hopefully move over to give me room.

QUINOA WITH SMOKED MACKEREL, SWEDE, PUNTARELLE, CELERY & MUSTARD KRAUT

Adapt this basic recipe according to what is in season.

INGREDIENTS

90g quinoa

250ml chicken stock or water

⅓ swede, cut into chunks

1 stick of celery

nubs of puntarelle or chicory

olive oil

red wine vinegar

smoked mackerel

a spoonful of mustard kraut, or other sauerkraut

salt and pepper

DIRECTIONS

Cook the quinoa in the chicken stock or water, adding a good pinch of flaky sea salt. If you're cooking a root vegetable, like today's swede, cook it in the same pot as the quinoa or steam it in a sieve over the pan, covered with a lid.

While it's cooking, prepare whatever other vegetables you'll be adding raw – today, it's celery and puntarelle – and make a vinaigrette from the oil and vinegar (if you have some chopped flat-leaf parsley to add, all the better). When the quinoa is cooked (usually after about 15 minutes, when all the liquid has been absorbed), put it in a serving bowl and add the raw vegetables.

Pull however much mackerel you want off the bone and add to the bowl, then add the kraut. Finish by adding the vinaigrette, and maybe some salt and pepper.

MADOKA AND OLA RINDAL

Les Restos du Coeur
France

Film stills by Ola Rindal, 2020

SILKA RITTSON-THOMAS

The Lemon Tree Trust
United Kingdom and United States

We have been spending the lockdown in our hamlet; we have started to deliver our flowers to the amazing Notting Hill Fish Shop where they are being sold. Since I have tired of cooking slightly, I bring in edibles from the gardens once a week to choose from during cooking. I pile them into an odd ceramic bust made by Stephen Claydon, which I bought a few years ago. I have never dared to use it functionally before as it's fragile and delicately balanced despite its imposing presence. I also take a load of edibles to London too for Anne and Chloe who work with me in the studio, prepping the flowers for the shop. They have become very resourceful, cooking with the produce I bring them and have made chive malfattis and wisteria infusions, delicious lilac meringues and sage butters.

ASPARAGUS ICE CREAM

The only puddings I know how to make and love making are ice creams and sorbets. I love asparagus and grow it madly so here is an asparagus ice cream, frozen in Victorian pewter ice cream moulds. The Victorians used all kinds of flavours in their ice creams with limitless imagination. The recipe comes from Kitty Travers's ice cream bible *La Grotta Ices* and is a version of her Pea Pod Ice Cream. Making the ice cream takes a bit of time as you need to cool the mix over night. If you make the ice cream without a machine, you need to stir it every hour until it's fully frozen.

INGREDIENTS
1 large bunch of asparagus
400ml whole milk
150ml double cream
a pinch of salt
4 egg yolks
130g sugar

DIRECTIONS
Shave the asparagus, chop into pieces and steam until tender. Heat the milk, cream and salt together in a pan, stirring occasionally. As soon as the liquid reaches simmering point, add the steamed asparagus and simmer for 4-5 minutes. Remove the pan from the heat and blitz the mix in a blender or a use stick blender.

Strain the mixture through a sieve, squeezing hard to extract as much flavour from the asparagus as possible, then discard the mash. Wash the pan and pour the fragrant milk and cream mixture back into it. Whisk the egg yolks and the sugar together in a separate bowl.

Bring the milk to a simmer, stirring often with a whisk or a spatula to prevent it from catching on the pan. Once the liquid is hot and steaming, start pouring it over the yolks in a thin stream, whisking continuously. Then return the whole mix to the pan and cook over a low heat until it reaches 82°C. If you don't have a digital thermometer, just make sure that it doesn't get as hot as boiling. Stir constantly to avoid curdling the eggs. Then take off the heat and plunge the base of the pan into a sink of iced water to cool down. Once the custard is at room temperature, scrape it into a clean container, cover and chill in the fridge overnight.

Pour the custard into an ice cream maker, churn according to the machine's instructions and then scrape into any container or into ice cream moulds lined with plastic film. If you don't have a machine, pour the custard into any container and place it in the freezer. Churn with a spatula once an hour until properly frozen.

MAX ROCHA

Community Food Hub
London, United Kingdom

Today, I am making shepherd's pie for my lunch, to lift the spirits on a wet Monday during Lockdown 3. I managed to get two lovely marrow bones from my butcher, alongside some nice lamb mince. This dish really reminds me of Ireland and it's so simple to make. The more rustic the better, I find.

Peas are a crucial element to a shepherd's pie for both colour and flavour. Even when they are not in season, I use frozen peas from my local shop. All the ingredients for this recipe came from my greengrocer, apart from the bits from the butcher. The key to a shepherd's pie is the mix of lamb mince and beef stock.

SHEPHERD'S PIE

INGREDIENTS

2 tablespoons olive oil

3 donkey carrots, chopped

2 onions, chopped

1 garlic clove, chopped

a few sprigs of thyme, picked and chopped

600g lamb mince

2 tablespoons tomato purée

2 tablespoons Worcestershire sauce

a splash of red wine (optional)

600ml beef stock

2 marrow bones

1 tablespoon Dijon mustard

300g frozen peas

800g potatoes, peeled

100g butter

a good splash of milk

a sprig of flat-leaf parsley

DIRECTIONS

Heat the olive oil in a heavy based pan and sweat down the carrot, onion and garlic for 5 minutes with the thyme. Turn the heat up, add the lamb mince and season with a little salt and pepper. Brown the mince and tip off any extra fat.

Add the tomato purée and Worcestershire sauce and allow to cook out for 5 more minutes. You can add a splash of red wine at this point if you have it. Then pour over your beef stock, mix well and place one of the whole marrow bones in too. Cover the pan and cook for 50 minutes, taking off the lid half way through. Remove the marrow bone, scrape the marrow out and mix into the mince with the mustard and peas.

Preheat a fan oven to 180°C. Place the other bone into the oven to par-cook. It should be ready by the time you have made the mash.

People have different ways of making mash, but this is my way. I boil the potatoes in salty water, then drain and mash with the butter and milk. My granny always heated up the milk every so slightly in a pan with the butter before adding to the mash, so that's how I do it. Season with salt and pepper.

Now place the mince in an ovenproof dish, nestle the bone from the oven in the middle of the dish and surround it with your beautiful mash. Bake in the oven until the mince is bubbling and the potato is getting a nice golden brown colour. Allow to sit for 10 minutes before serving with a sprig of parsley in the bone marrow.

ROKSANDA

Hackney Foodbank and Dinner is Served
London, United Kingdom

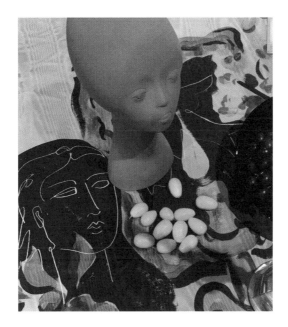

SERBIAN BREAD (POGAČA)

Rather than the traditional pogača often used for celebrations, I've adapted the recipe to a more everyday style, choosing dark rye and a touch of walnut for flavour.

INGREDIENTS
1 sachet of dried yeast
310ml warm water
2 teaspoons salt
1 tablespoon sugar
2 tablespoons oil
350g dark rye flour
a handful of walnuts

DIRECTIONS
Dissolve the yeast in the warm water in a large bowl. Add the salt, sugar and oil and stir until completely mixed. Add the flour and walnuts and mix until a cohesive dough forms. Knead until smooth. Place the dough in a greased bowl, cover and let rise in a warm place until doubled in size.

Heat the oven to 180°C. Turn the dough out onto a lightly floured surface and shape into a flat round. Transfer to a baking sheet lined with parchment paper. Prick the loaf all over with a fork and rub the top of the bread with oil or sugar dissolved in water. Let stand, uncovered, for 15 minutes in a warm place.

Bake the bread for 30 minutes or until an instant-read thermometer registers 90°C. The loaf should sound hollow when tapped. Let cool completely on a wire rack before cutting.

KUBA RYNIEWICZ

Newcastle West End Foodbank
Newcastle-upon-Tyne, United Kingdom

Alice Rout photographed by Kuba Ryniewicz, 2021

SILESIAN DUMPLINGS

Making Silesian dumplings is a messy kind of fun. The origins of this simple yet fulfilling dish lie in a region in the south of Poland with a strong identity – Silesia (Ślask).

INGREDIENTS
1kg potatoes, peeled
100g potato flour
1–2 eggs
a sprinkle of regular flour
1 onion, chopped
a few mushrooms, sliced
a small handful of pancetta (optional)
olive oil
salt and pepper
gherkins (as many as you need), to serve

DIRECTIONS
Firstly boil the potatoes until tender, cool them a little then mash while still warm. Add the potato flour, eggs, salt and pepper and mix it all with your hands until it forms a smooth but gluey dough. Form the dough into small round shapes the size of eggs or passion fruit. Then press them so they look like mini doughnuts. During this process you may get frustrated as the dough can stick to your hands, so sprinkle some regular flour on the table and your hands to make life easier.

Boil water in a large pot and drop the dumplings individually into the water. Cook for up to 2 minutes – as soon as they start floating on the surface of the water, you know they are cooked.

Get another pan and fry the onions, mushrooms and pancetta (if you are using it) in some olive oil. Add the cooked dumplings to the pan and fry for a couple of minutes to make them slightly crispy. Season and serve with gherkins.

BIANCA SAUNDERS

Black Minds Matter
United Kingdom

MAC & CHEESE

INGREDIENTS

500g macaroni
olive oil
1 teaspoon paprika
1 tablespoon all-purpose seasoning
1 onion, diced
2 garlic cloves, chopped
250ml milk
125ml double cream
600g mature Cheddar cheese, grated
200g Red Leicester cheese, grated
2 tablespoons breadcrumbs
1 teaspoon finely chopped parsley
salt and black pepper

DIRECTIONS

Fill a large saucepan with water and bring to the boil. Season with salt then add the pasta and cook for 7–9 minutes.

Heat a tablespoon of olive oil in a small pan over a medium heat, season with salt, 1 teaspoon of black pepper, the paprika and all purpose seasoning and cook for a few minutes, then set aside.

Heat a dash of olive oil in another pan over a medium heat, add the onion and garlic and cook gently until soft and caramelized. Season to taste then add the milk, cream and 400g of the Cheddar and bring to the boil. Allow to bubble away and thicken.

Once the pasta is cooked, drain it and return to the pan, add the spiced oil and mix well. Then pour the cheese sauce over the pasta and mix again. Pour the pasta into an oven tray, top with the Red Leicester and remaining Cheddar along with the breadcrumbs, then sprinkle with the parsley. Place in the oven on a medium heat for 20 minutes until it is golden brown and bubbling. Serve while hot!

GIOCONDA SCOTT

Fundación Banco de Alimentos de Sevilla
Seville, Spain

A DELICIOUS SPRING TORTILLA

INGREDIENTS

5 medium potatoes

4 or 5 small spring onions with ½ the green removed

4 large eggs

about 250ml extra virgin olive oil

¼ teaspoon ground turmeric

leaves from a few sprigs of mint, torn

sea salt

DIRECTIONS

Peel the potatoes and cut into quarters lengthways, then slice across into 7mm wedges. Put them into a colander and mix with a good pinch of salt to help them release their moisture. Medium slice the onions and beat the eggs in a large bowl.

Pour 2–3cm of olive oil into a deep, heavy based frying pan about 25cm in diameter, then heat until hot but not smoking. Pat the potatoes dry and pour them into the pan. Fry for a few minutes until lightly golden and beginning to soften, then add the onion. Continue to cook until all is soft and golden. Remove from the oil with a slotted spoon and put into a colander to cool for a few minutes before adding the mixture to the beaten eggs. At this point, I add the turmeric and torn mint leaves. Mix all the ingredients together well, taste and season accordingly.

Use a clean nonstick frying pan and pour in a little of the oil used to fry the potatoes. You want to just cover the bottom of the pan. Heat over a high heat until the oil is hot but not smoking, then pour in the potato/egg mixture. Allow the bottom of the tortilla to seal, then turn the heat down to cook the tortilla about two-thirds through. (Give it a little shake to make sure it doesn't get stuck.) You are now going to flip the tortilla over, so you want to make sure that it is not too runny on top.

Put a lid or plate over the frying pan that generously covers the top. Hold the pan quite firmly and flip the pan over, turning the tortilla onto the lid or plate. (You will need some practice with this, but the more you do it, the easier it will get.) Now slide the tortilla back into the pan. Give it a little shake and tuck in any edges that may have displaced themselves.

To finish, turn the heat quite high again to seal it on the other side for about 30 seconds. Then turn the heat down and leave for another minute or so. (Give it a little shake again.) Now flip the tortilla again to make sure you have the right colour underneath. Slide onto a plate and eat.

In Spain there are many variations of this dish. The potato and the egg are the staples – you can add any combination of ingredients to them. I like this particular mix.

FANNY SINGER

The Edible Schoolyard Project
Berkeley, United States

COMING HOME PASTA

There are a few things or, I should say, a few dishes, that I associate with coming home after a long period away. The main one, of course, is Coming Home Pasta. Whenever my family left for a stretch of weeks – what, as a child, resembled an eternity – we would come home to our strange-feeling house and immediately set about orienting ourselves through food. To be fair, we oriented ourselves through food whatever the place, the time, the country or the continent, but the fact that such an orientation felt necessary, even at home, I think does speak for our family's particular brand of devotion.

I can very distinctly remember the feeling of coming home to the Berkeley house after a long trip. As we spilled through the front door, the house would creak under our luggage as if, in our absence, it had grown unaccustomed to the weight both of us and our cargo. The house smelled a bit stale and of dust, always, a scent amplified by the ancient floor heaters as they were switched on and began to roast the particles accumulated after so many weeks of disuse.

We always seemed to be returning after nightfall, and so these memories of nostos (a bit of Homerian vocabulary feels warranted here) are tinged with the inky hue of night, or rather have since taken on a fuzzy, wine-dark haze, much like the colour Homer paints of the Odyssean seas. And indeed it was always a moment for opening a bottle of wine, usually red, because that meant that no one had to have remembered to chill it before leaving. Plucked from the cellar, it could be counted on to immediately slake parental thirst. One or the other guardian (or Bob) would descend through the trapdoor in the kitchen floor – an architectural feature I am so used to as to be inured to its eccentricity, though this detail is never lost on new visitors to the house – and proceed to the musty-smelling cellar below where, during my father's tenure at least, a very considerable wine inventory was stored.

No one unpacked. Rather a wordless series of actions was set into motion: the putting on of a pot of water to boil, the burning of a parched rosemary branch left out in the basket on the table (our family's incense), the lighting of a candle, the rustling in the pantry drawers for a bag of pasta, opened or unopened – it didn't matter. I was usually dispatched to the garden with a flashlight to pick a few handfuls of herbs. This generally meant parsley, sometimes a bit of oregano – only the herbs that could withstand a good stretch of neglect and whose flavour didn't change too much if they'd mostly gone to seed. Sending me out into the dark of the back garden had the added benefit of giving my mom a brief window in which to quickly extract a few anchovies from under salt in their container in the fridge and add them to the sauce (if you could even call the frugal dressing characteristic of Coming Home Pasta a sauce). I would have baulked at their inclusion; once anchovies were incorporated into a dish and decently disguised, however, I would eat them contentedly.

Other things were rummaged for: some still-firm cloves of garlic to mince and fry in oil in the gleaming blue-black lap of my mother's favourite cast iron pan; some chilli flakes to join the garlic there in its hot oil shimmy. The smell of the house would begin to transform. There was reliably a nubbin of ancient Parmesan in the fridge, blooming with pale age spots but unspoiled. It would taste fine, even good, grated and married with the other heady flavours of garlic and chilli and herbs and anchovy and sometimes a handful of coarsely chopped salt-packed capers, whose flavour was pleasantly abrupt and tangy. Sea salt, black pepper and a good, voluptuous pour of olive oil at the end. This was Coming Home Pasta. We ate this concoction in relative silence. The darkness made it seem frivolous to switch on music; conversation felt redundant after so many hours trapped together in transit. So we twirled our next-to-naked noodles and ate to know that we had made it – made it back home again to the table.

Making Coming Home Pasta scarcely requires more articulation of method than I've already given it – it is very open to interpretation and should be adapted to whatever you have on hand. Alice Trillin, the very beloved wife of Calvin 'Bud' Trillin – the man I think of as my Jewish godfather, though I realise that's a contradiction in terms – wrote me a not-dissimilar recipe called Lonely Girl Pasta for *Fanny's Exclusive College Survival Cookbook*, the book my parents and Bob presented to me as a high school graduation gift. Alice submitted her recipe the year she passed away, and I've always felt more than a pang of sadness reading over its gentle and pragmatic instructions and economical ingredients. Still, I believe her recipe presumed the presence of at least a pepper or broccoli floret in the refrigerator, still fresh enough to merit inclusion. Such was not the case in our house, both because peppers and broccoli were generally frowned upon (I think my mom associated them with the insipid canned vegetables of her youth) and because her obsession with voiding the icebox of its contents prior to our departure bordered on compulsion. Her close friends and I tease her that one of her biggest pet peeves is an abundantly stocked fridge.

But despite the spareness of the ingredients and the unfussiness of the preparation, this is in fact a delicious pasta recipe. The Italians – progenitors of time-tested dishes whose names are nice-sounding translations of things as uncomplicated as 'cheese and pepper' (*cacio e pepe*), 'garlic, oil and chilli' (*aglio, olio e peperoncino*), and 'tomato' (*al pomodoro*) – can be trusted on this subject: often the best-tasting dishes are the simplest. The second you walk through the door, put the water on to boil. Even if it comes to a boil before you've gathered your wits or prepared the other components, there's something about a pot

of simmering water that immediately lends atmosphere to a room and imparts a sense of homeliness. Salt the water abundantly. Locate whatever leftover, desultory dry pasta you may have in your pantry. If you are feeding more than one person and have a little bit of three kinds and not enough of any one, boil three separate pots of water. (Do not be tempted, as I often have, to boil different shapes or types of pasta in the same pot; it's a guaranteed disaster of under- and overdoneness.) I don't mind combining the varieties afterwards so long as they're all more or less the same species, although this admission no doubt amounts to some form of

sacrilege – just try not to mix a short, fat fusilli with a long, thin linguine, for example.

Garlic – garlic is the next most important ingredient. Yes, this pasta can be made with an onion instead – that lesser allium – diced and softened in olive oil in a pan, but garlic is the flavour that I think most brings you back into yourself, most provokes that necessary feeling of re-embodiment after a period of travel. Still, use the garlic only if its cloves are very firm and shiny once unsheathed, and the smell, when sliced open, is peppery and fresh and not at all dusty or stale. Mince the garlic (the more cloves the merrier) and fry in

a heavy based pan in a good glug of olive oil. Once the garlic starts to smell fragrant, add a few pinches of chilli, if you like spice, and then a couple of chopped anchovy fillets (the best I've ever tasted – and this from a former sceptic—are the high-quality Spanish varieties packed in olive oil). A few chopped capers are also welcome at this stage, but be sure to rinse them if they've been kept in salt. Be careful that the garlic never begins to brown or burn while your attention is elsewhere. Turn off the flame immediately if it starts to migrate in that direction.

Your pasta should be al dente, both because the toothiness of the noodles in some way compensates for the slightness of other ingredients, but also because you will be coming home hungry from a trip and will want to remove the noodles at the first possible moment. Heed this impulse. Use a spider or tongs to transfer the pasta directly into your frying pan, adding a bit of the salted cooking water if you feel it needs lubrication. Grate a generous amount of Parmesan into the pan and add a handful of chopped parsley if you have fresh herbs in your garden or in a window box. Correct with extra olive oil, a squeeze of lemon and a generous showering of zest, a pinch of salt, or some ground pepper, if necessary. When it tastes just right, yell out, 'À table!' as my mother did before every single meal, as if calling not just her child, but the whole neighbourhood, to the table. There's always enough food for one more.

INGREDIENTS

Pasta of any shape or size, fresh or dried, cooked al dente according to the instructions on the packet

LOTS of minced garlic (a whole head!)

Chopped head of flat-leaf parsley (and any other herbs you'd like that will go nicely: oregano, coriander...)

1 lemon, juice and zest

Grated Parmesan

Black pepper

Sea salt

Red chilli flakes or fresh minced red bird's eye chilli

Anchovies (optional)

Salt-packed capers (optional)

Embroider with whatever you have! Sautéed mushrooms, roughly chiffonaded kale, pitted olives, caramelized diced onions or shallots, and so on.

JOSEFINE SKOMARS & ANNA NEVALA

City Harvest London
London, United Kingdom

Anna and I moved in together during the first London lockdown. Unable to spend long lazy park lunches under the spring sun, we often brought the flower meadow into our kitchen doing what we do when we feel the need to break up the everyday: set the floor for an indoor picnic.

We are both from Finland and to soothe the homesickness this past year we've made dishes from back home. A festive favourite of ours is the savoury layered cake – *smörgåstårta* in Swedish, *voileipäkakku* in Finnish, which translates as sandwich cake. In Finland there is seldom a celebration or major life event without a sandwich cake on the table: birthdays, graduations, funerals. This recipe is a simple version that has been adapted from both of our family recipes and has now found a place in our very own London family recipe book. All non-vegan ingredients can be replaced with their vegan equivalents, if you prefer.

SANDWICH CAKE

INGREDIENTS

24 slices of brown bread, cut into squares,
　　crusts trimmed
vegetable stock, for wetting
cream cheese, for spreading

FILLING

4 tins of tuna in brine, drained
200ml sweet and sour pickles, finely chopped
400ml crème fraîche
200ml mayonnaise
4 tablespoons lemon juice
1 tangy apple, grated
fresh dill, chopped
salt and pepper

DIRECTIONS

Mix all the filling ingredients in a large bowl. Add dill, salt and pepper to taste. Start layering the cake with a layer of bread. We shaped our cake as a square with four pieces of bread per layer. Wet the edges of the bread with vegetable stock and spread a layer of filling evenly between each layer of bread. Finish with one last bread layer and cover the cake with cream cheese. We decorated ours with pea shoots, redcurrants, blackberries, radishes, dill, cucumber and figs. Use whatever is in season and tickles your imagination.

LEXIE SMITH

Meals For Good
New York City, United States

This is a recipe for my spiral flatbreads. Read the directions below, but adjust the recipe as you wish – it's pretty flexible. If you want to leave out the leavening altogether, try it and see what happens – the result will be different but still worthwhile (steam will do a lot of the lifting). Want to avoid the stovetop labour? Heat a pizza stone or baking sheet up to 250°C in the oven and bake a few breads on it at a time for a couple minutes, until just poofed. Don't have beetroot? Whatever, use a different vegetable purée or just make the white dough. No wholegrain flour? Replace with more plain white and use a little less liquid. No milk? Use all water. You are your own master.

UPWARD SPIRAL FLATBREADS

INGREDIENTS

WHITE DOUGH
190g plain flour
85g wholegrain spelt or wholegrain flour
7g salt
55g milk
55g water
90g yoghurt
55g sourdough starter (active or discard)

PINK DOUGH
115g beetroot purée (see below)
olive oil
190g plain flour
85g wholegrain spelt or wholegrain flour
7g salt
55g milk
55g water
55g sourdough starter (active or discard)

DIRECTIONS
To make the beetroot purée, you'll need 2 smallish beetroot. Leave them whole if petite and reasonably sized, or cut in half if they're as big as a fist or bigger. Rub in olive oil, wrap individually in foil and bake in a hot oven, around 200°C, for a couple of hours. Let them sit until at least cool enough to handle, then remove from the foil and rub the skins off with the sides of your thumbs. Blend in a food processor until smooth. Set aside 115g for the dough.

If you're using active sourdough starter instead of discard, feed it around 3 hours before you plan to mix the dough. Take your wet ingredients out of the refrigerator, assuming that's where they live, and let them sit at room temperature for an hour or two before mixing.

You'll be making two separate but very similar doughs. Start by weighing out all the dry ingredients in two mixing bowls. Now add the milk, water and yoghurt to the white dough bowl; and the milk, water and beetroot purée to the pink dough bowl. Mix both doughs, one at a time, until just combined. Cover the bowls and leave for 30–90 minutes. (This step is about hydrating the flour so the dough can begin forming its gluten structure. It's called an autolyse.)

Choose a dough to start with, white or pink, and mix the sourdough starter in, kneading thoroughly with the palm and heel of your hand (a tip: moistening your hands prevents dough from sticking to them). You can begin mixing in the bowl and then move to a work surface once the sourdough is relatively incorporated. I mostly use a single hand for this process: press on the dough with the heel of your hand and fold it over itself. Turn and repeat. Do this again and again until it begins to smooth itself out. Also consider the Slap and Fold: an audacious but real name for a certain hand-mixing technique, accomplished by slapping the dough onto the work surface from above, pulling the edge up and towards you, and then folding it over itself. Tug it back up from the work surface by its side (the edge of your hand below your pinky finger should be on the work surface, not your knuckles), slap down again, tug up, fold and so on. Watch a video (mine?) and you'll get it. Try it yourself and you'll really get it.

Continue kneading for a few minutes, then round the dough into a ball, grease with olive oil and let rest. If the dough was still tearing easily, give it another few slap and folds after a 5 minute break (firm but gentle). Do all of this with the second dough too. Once they're nicely developed and smooth, rest both doughs in separate bowls greased generously with olive oil. Cover and let sit at room temperature for one hour, then refrigerate the doughs overnight.

The next day, remove the doughs from the fridge. Place them both upside down on a well-floured work surface. Roll each dough out to a rectangle about 0.5cm thick, dusting lightly with flour as needed to prevent sticking. Place the white dough gently on top of the pink dough (draping over a floured rolling pin to help transport, if needed). Starting from one of the shorter edges of the rectangle, roll up into a log.

Use a very sharp or serrated knife (not to say a serrated knife shouldn't also be very sharp – it should – but who can really tell with serrated knives?), and slice confidently into 14–16 pieces, a generous 1cm thick. Place the slices cut side down on a floured surface. One by one, flour and roll out the pieces into rounds about 0.25cm thick and about 12cm wide (this will vary). Cover with a towel or plastic wrap as you go to prevent drying out.

Heat a cast iron pan or equally hearty cooking surface up to hot, hot (high heat). Make sure it has a few minutes to really get there (I get it going after rolling out around half the batch and let it heat up while I finish). Once some

water (or spit, really, if we're being honest and not giving these breads away) sizzles and evaporates immediately after hitting the surface, you're ready. Start with the first round you rolled out and slap it onto the pan, as if it's actually a cheek you're slapping (either kind). Count to about 20 and flip (use your hands if you're me or a metal spatula if you're smart). You know it's ready to turn when you see little bubbles forming on the surface. Once flipped, the new top should already have some brown or golden marks on it. If not, your pan needs a bit more heat.

Wait another 20 or so seconds and flip again. Then again. Hold on a sec. At this point you may get some poofing action. You'll know it when you see it, oh will you ever. Sometimes the steam that's filling the pocket of the bread can be coaxed around by applying pressure on the dough with a folded cloth (careful here – steam is hot). Keep flipping, pressing.

Remove from the heat when the surface is mottled with brown marks and all the sheen of the raw dough is gone. Wrap in a kitchen towel immediately. Dousing with some ghee or olive oil while hot doesn't hurt. Cook them all and freeze or share as needed.

NOTES

Not all the breads will poof. But when they do, god, it's all worth it. Pocket bread's behaviour is something of a mystery, but there is a hazy road map. They are more likely to poof if: the surface of the dough round is smooth and has no nicks or tears before getting into the pan, the round is not too thick nor too thin and is a consistent width throughout, and the pan is good and hot and kept that way.

You don't want to over-brown these; it will make them tough and stale faster. So if one of your breads is not poofing…I know the hurt, but you can't wait forever.

If you find they're charring very quickly, turn the heat to medium or medium-high for a minute or two. This will probably be necessary after you've made about half the batch and the pan has been working for a while. Remember to turn it back up after some time if the breads seem like they're moving sluggishly.

The more of a pocket you achieve, the more tender the breads will be, but either way they're a delight. But tenderness is a very worthy goal to strive towards.

MONIKA SPRÜTH

Berliner Engel Für Bedürftige
Berlin, Germany

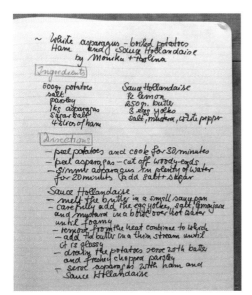

~ White asparagus - boiled potatoes
Ham and sauce Hollandaise
by Monika + Paolina

[Ingredients]

500gr. potatoes   Sauce Hollandaise
salt   ½ lemon
parsley   250 gr. butter
1kg asparagus   3 egg yolks
sugar salt   salt, mustard, white pepper
4 slices of ham

[Directions]

- peel potatoes and cook for 30 minutes
- peel asparagus - cut off woody ends
- simmer asparagus in plenty of water
  for 20 minutes add salt + sugar

Sauce Hollandaise
- melt the butter in a small saucepan
- carefully add the egg yolks, salt, lemon juice
  and mustard in a bowl over hot water
  until foamy
- remove from the heat continue to whisk
- add the butter in a thin stream until
  it is glossy
- drain the potatoes serve with butter
  and freshly chopped parsley
- serve asparagus with ham and
  Sauce Hollandaise

WANNSEE

During lockdown in Berlin, we cooked *Wannsee*, a very traditional German dish of the season and of the region. Here, in the area around Berlin, the soil is very sandy and the famous thick asparagus Beelitzer Spargel is grown. The season runs from April till June, the same as the fresh strawberries we also have here.

Originally, we wanted to cook another German dish, *Königsberger Klopse* (meatballs in creamy caper sauce), but the asparagus season has just started and I am in the middle of the sandy soil of Brandenburg so I thought white asparagus would be more fitting. I am in lockdown with my daughter Paolina, who is half Italian and half German. I am fully Prussian/German and we are sticking to very simple home cooking using German and Italian recipes, which I have written out in a little cookbook.

ANNA TOBIAS

AAA: Ambition Aspire Achieve
London, United Kingdom

This recipe is based on a risotto I learned how to cook while working at the River Café; it has been adapted for lockdown. I can remember being initially very sceptical about the idea of a tomato risotto, then had to eat humble pie on tasting it as it really is delicious. In many ways, it shouldn't have come as a surprise to someone who used to love eating boiled rice with ketchup as a child, but I'd obviously become a bit pompous as a young chef! Use the white wine if you have it – I wouldn't bother opening a bottle of wine just for this, unless you plan to drink the rest anyway.

TINNED TOMATO RISOTTO

INGREDIENTS

80g butter

a glug of olive oil

1 onion, finely chopped

2 sticks of celery, finely chopped (not a disaster if you don't have this)

2 garlic cloves, finely chopped

2 small sprigs of rosemary, finely chopped

1 tin of tomatoes

350g risotto rice (such as carnaroli or arborio)

100ml white wine (optional)

1 litre stock (I used chicken stock that I had in the freezer)

40g grated Parmesan, plus extra for grating at the end

salt and pepper

DIRECTIONS

Melt 50g of the butter in a pan with the glug of olive oil. Add the onion, celery, garlic and rosemary. Sweat gently until completely soft and cooked. Add the tin of tomatoes, season with salt and pepper (and possibly half a teaspoon of sugar if your tin of tomatoes is a bit acidic) and simmer for about 25 minutes.

Next add the rice. I realise that I am not doing the 'frying the rice' part in the usual way, but I promise this works well. (My admission is that when I made this, I didn't want to make the sauce separately so I could save on the amount of washing up!) Cook the rice with the tomato sauce on quite a high heat for a few minutes, then add the wine if you have it.

Now add a ladle of hot stock to the rice and stir constantly while maintaining a gentle simmer. Once the first ladle has been absorbed by the rice, continue adding ladles of stock and stirring until the rice is cooked but still has a little bite. Make sure the consistency is relatively loose – it should be able to slide slowly down a plate if you tilt it, not stick to it. Add more stock if necessary to achieve this consistency.

Finally, add the grated Parmesan and remaining butter and adjust the seasoning as necessary. Stir into the rice and then allow to settle for a minute before serving with a final grating of Parmesan on top. Serves 4 as a main course.

TESSA TRAEGER & PATRICK KINMONTH

St Mungo's
London, United Kingdom

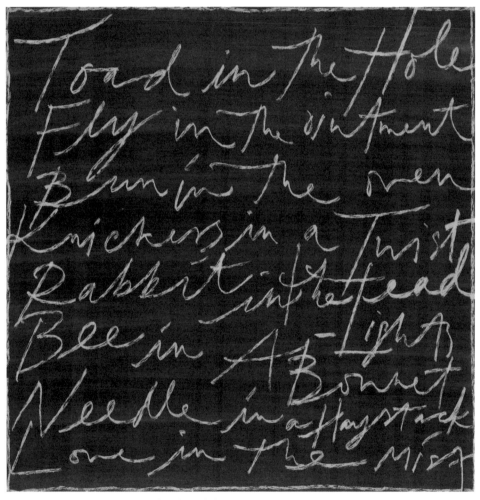

Toad in the Hole by Patrick Kinmonth, 2021

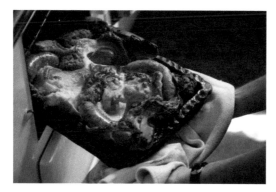

Photograph by Tessa Traeger, 2021

TOAD IN THE HOLE

This is the perfect lunch on a cold winter day. You will need proper organic sausages from your butcher as supermarket sausages can be too watery with thin skins.

INGREDIENTS
2 eggs, lightly beaten
300ml milk
100g plain flour
a pinch of salt
6 butcher's sausages
dripping, oil or butter, for frying
Worcestershire sauce

DIRECTIONS
Beat the eggs and milk together in a jug. Sieve the flour and salt into a bowl and stir in half the egg and milk mixture slowly, bit by bit. Once you have a smooth paste with no lumps, add the rest of the liquid and beat for 5-10 minutes. Put the batter aside for an hour or two.

The Aga needs to be fully up to temperature, or preheat your oven to its highest setting. The secret of a good toad in the hole is a really hot oven which makes the batter rise properly. You can use a roasting tin or a ceramic ovenproof dish but whatever you use, it should have gently sloping sides so that the batter can rise smoothly up. Put your dish or tin in the oven to heat.

Meanwhile, fry the sausages in dripping or a mixture of oil and butter for about 10 minutes until they are brown on both sides but only half cooked. Now take the dish or tin out of the oven, arrange the sausages in it and rapidly pour in the batter all around the sausages so that they rise gently above the mixture. At this stage I like to sprinkle Worcestershire sauce over the batter. Close the oven and cook for 30-40 minutes, until the batter has risen and is crispy brown underneath. Serve immediately as otherwise the batter will collapse.

KITTY TRAVERS

The Lemon Tree Trust
United Kingdom and United States

As an alternative to lollies, I've also been freezing this ice cream in individual glasses with a squeeze of lime juice over the top and eating them straight from the freezer. The lime juice freezes into an icy and acidic layer and tastes like a Wall's Twister. For some funny reason, the contrast makes it much more delicious than if you were to mix the lime juice in with the rest of the ingredients. This recipe makes about 1 litre of ice cream.

MANGO ICE CREAM LOLLIES

INGREDIENTS
450g freshly sliced Alphonse mango flesh
a pinch of sea salt
150g coconut cream
150g double cream
200g sweetened condensed milk
finely grated zest of 1 lime
150g bitter chocolate
1 tablespoon coconut oil
150g desiccated coconut, lightly toasted in a
    dry pan

DIRECTIONS
Place all the ingredients, except the chocolate, coconut oil and desiccated coconut, in the fridge for 2–3 hours before starting. Blend the mango, salt, both creams and the condensed milk together with the lime zest until very smooth, then pass the mixture through a fine sieve.

Pour the cold mixture into an ice cream machine and churn according to the machine's instructions until frozen and the texture of whipped cream – about 25 minutes. Decant the ice cream into individual silicone lolly moulds, place a lolly stick into each one and hard-freeze overnight.

The following day, melt the chocolate and the coconut oil in a bowl over a small pan of very gently simmering water (make sure the bowl doesn't touch the water). Stir until smooth and liquid then remove from the pan.

Pop out each lolly and dip into the melted chocolate. Allow to drip for a few seconds before rolling in toasted coconut. Place on a sheet of baking parchment then return the lollies to the freezer for an hour or so. Store the lollies in a lidded container; they will keep very well for a week or two.

ANAÏS VAN MANEN

University College Hospital Macmillan Cancer Centre
London, United Kingdom

Making bread is often seen as a time-consuming hobby as it needs to prove and rise – definitely not something one would make for lunch. I really wanted to challenge that notion and make a delicious dish in under an hour with flatbreads made from scratch. You can make this with soy yoghurt if you prefer. Every component of the dish is versatile – you can enjoy the green yoghurt with raw vegetables, or the flatbreads with other fillings.

SPICED FLATBREAD, GREEN YOGHURT & SPRING GREENS

INGREDIENTS

200g plain flour

½ teaspoon salt

½ teaspoon sugar

½ teaspoon ground turmeric

¼ teaspoon paprika

a pinch of cumin seeds

1¼ teaspoons baking powder

¼ red onion, finely chopped

a handful of chopped fresh coriander

2 tablespoons yoghurt

1 tablespoon olive oil, plus extra for cooking

75ml water

a large handful of greens, such as purple sprouting broccoli or spring cabbage

a pinch of dried chilli flakes

a squeeze of lemon juice

Green yoghurt (see below)

chopped pistachios, to sprinkle

DIRECTIONS

Mix the flour, salt, sugar, spices and baking powder together in one mixing bowl, and the onion, coriander, yoghurt, oil and water together in another. Pour the wet ingredients into the dry ingredients and mix. Form into a slightly sticky dough and bring together into a ball. Cover the bowl and let it rest for 10–15 minutes.

Preheat your oven to 60-70°C. In a hot pan, add a dash of olive oil and sear your greens all over. Season then cover the pan to allow the steam to cook the veg. You want it charred but tender. Season with more sea salt if needed, a tiny pinch of chilli flakes and good squeeze of lemon juice. Keep your greens warm in the oven while you cook the flatbreads.

Dust a work surface with flour or a mixture of polenta and flour (the polenta will give a crunchy feel to your flatbreads). Divide your dough into four balls and roll them out to about 3-4mm thick, dusting with flour if they're too sticky to handle.

Place a pan over medium heat until hot but not smoking hot, add 1-2 tablespoons of oil and carefully place a flatbread in the pan. Cook until golden on one side, then flip onto the other side – roughly 1-2 minutes per side. I like to brush my bread with extra virgin olive oil or butter as soon as it comes out of the pan. Repeat with the other flatbreads.

Spread green yoghurt on top of your warm flatbread and add your cooked veg. Finish with some chopped pistachios and chilli flakes. If you have chilli oil, feel free to drizzle some as well. Serves 2.

GREEN YOGHURT

INGREDIENTS

6 heaped tablespoons yoghurt

2 tablespoons olive oil

20 shelled pistachios

4 spring onions

1 avocado

2 handfuls of fresh coriander

2 teaspoons honey or maple syrup

4 teaspoons almond butter

1 garlic clove

salt and black pepper

DIRECTIONS

Place all the ingredients in a blender and blend until smooth.

Painting by Magda Archer for Poot It In Yer Bag, 2021
Read more about the Poot It In Yer Bag project on page 32.

SOPHIE VON HELLERMANN & JONATHAN VYNER

Our Kitchen
Margate, United Kingdom

Cheesy Leeks painted by Sophie von Hellermann, 2020

OYSTERS & CHEESY LEEKS

The following lunch of oysters and cheesy leeks was created by Jonathan Vyner in the home he shares with artist Sophie von Hellermann in Margate in 2020.

Oysters from around here, with white wine vinegar and chopped shallots
1 lemon (optional, we didn't have any)
Cheesy leeks with ham
Shredded carrot salad with shallots and parsley, oils and vinegar
Sourdough bread

GARETH WRIGHTON

Watford Foodbank
Watford, United Kingdom

GRILLED GOATS' CHEESE & CHERRY COMPOTE SANDWICH

INGREDIENTS
2 slices of your favourite bread
a knob of butter
a drop of olive oil
slices of goats' cheese
Savoury Cherry Compote (see below)

DIRECTIONS
Toast and butter both slices of bread. Place one slice, butter side down, in a frying pan over a medium-high heat with a drop of olive oil. Immediately turn the heat to low. While the bottom layer browns, stack up as much goats' cheese as you want on it and top with cherry compote. Then top with the final slice of toast, butter side up. Press down with a spatula. Just as the goats' cheese starts to go south, flip the sandwich as best you can, and cook the other side until it is also crisp and brown. Enjoy!

SAVOURY CHERRY COMPOTE

This compote goes well with duck, pork chops, sausages on toast, or in a grilled cheese sandwich as above.

INGREDIENTS
2 small shallots, finely diced
2 teaspoons olive oil
1 large punnet of cherries, stoned, or a bag of frozen cherries
1 teaspoon finely chopped fresh rosemary
1 teaspoon balsamic vinegar
1 teaspoon honey
250ml sherry, kirsch or water

DIRECTIONS
Fry the shallots in the olive oil in a large pan over a low heat until translucent. Add the cherries, rosemary, balsamic vinegar and honey and stir until all is slick in the oil. Cook through over a medium heat. Just as they start to catch on the bottom of the pan, deglaze with sherry, kirsch or water. Reduce and cook off any alcohol.

Keep on a medium-low heat until the cherries are completely cooked through and their juice has stained the shallots. Top up with water and cook down further if the pan gets too dry. The cherries should be soft and collapse easily when you press them with the back of a spoon. Leave to cool and store in a jar in the fridge.

EDITOR AND PUBLISHER
Frances von Hofmannsthal
Nominated organisation: Edible London, United Kingdom

MANAGING EDITOR
Josefine Skomars
Nominated organisation: City Harvest London, United Kingdom

ART DIRECTORS
Giulia Garbin and Mariana Sameiro
Nominated organisation: Frati Cappuccini in Montuzza, Trieste, Italy
Nominated organisation: Banco Alimentar Contra a Fome, Portugal

EDITORIAL AND PRODUCTION
Sophie Kullmann
Nominated organisation: Independent Food Aid Network, United Kingdom

Texts and Images © The Authors
(unless otherwise stated)
For the book in this form © LUNCHEON magazine Ltd.
All rights reserved. No part of this publication may be reproduced in whole
or part without written permission from the publisher.

Printed by Westerham, United Kingdom, on Munken Polar (by Arctic paper)
which is FSC and EU Ecolabel certified. Munken is an environmentally
friendly and ecologically sound paper produced at Munkedals in Sweden,
which is one of the world's cleanest fine paper mills.

FSC
www.fsc.org
FSC® C020637
The mark of
responsible forestry

ISBN: 9780993542305

Back cover: *Banana in a Handbag* by Thelma Speirs for Poot It In Yer Bag, 2021
Read more about the Poot It In Yer Bag project on page 32.

PUBLISHED BY
LUNCHEON EDITIONS, 2021